S0-EGE-062

INTERMEDIATE PIANO REPERTOIRE

A GUIDE FOR TEACHING

Third Edition

Cathy Albergo
Professor of Music
William Rainey Harper College
Palatine, Illinois

Reid Alexander
Professor of Music
University of Illinois
Urbana, Illinois

The Frederick Harris Music Co., Limited

FREDERICK
HARRIS
MUSIC

Canadian Cataloguing in Publication Data

Albergo, Cathy, 1951-
    Intermediate piano repertoire : a guide for teaching

ISBN 0-88797-375-2

1. Piano music - Bibliography. 2. Piano music -
Bibliography - Graded lists. I. Alexander, Reid, 1949-
II. Title.

ML128.P3A5 1993   016.7862   C93-094847-5

Cover Design by Falcom Design and Communications

© Copyright 1993 The Frederick Harris Music Co., Limited
Oakville, Ontario, Canada. All Rights Reserved

Printed in Canada

Table of Contents

Foreword to the Third Edition

The piano teaching profession has been without a book for too long that focuses on the large body of intermediate level piano repertoire. We have to wait no longer--it is here in this volume: *Intermediate Piano Repertoire: A Guide for Teaching.*

Numerous books have partially addressed this subject. The Kern-Titus *The Teacher's Guidebook to Piano Literature* (1954), aimed at the college non-keyboard major, was divided into eight semesters of study (four years of undergraduate study), and listed suggested repertoire for each semester. No annotations were included, only titles, composers and publishers. Ernest Hutchinson's *The Literature of the Piano* (1948), revised by Rudolph Ganz (1964), touched on intermediate repertoire but only peripherally. The Friskin-Freundlich *Music for the Piano* (1954) included some of this repertoire but basically covered the period 1590-1952 and was organized by periods and style groupings. F. E. Kirby's *Short History of Keyboard Music* (1966) covered some of this material although it was musicologically oriented. My own *Guide to the Pianist's Repertoire* (1973), revised and enlarged edition (1987), looked at the important solo piano literature and answered the questions, What is it like? and Where can I get it? Some intermediate repertoire was included.

But now we have a book that concentrates entirely on this wonderful body of literature that provides the step to the great music written for our instrument. Many readers will be surprised to learn how much intermediate repertoire was composed by some of our 19th-century greats like Chopin and Liszt as well as current 20th-century educational composers. Both authors are authorities in the intermediate repertoire area; both teach piano pedagogy and practicum courses, and have worked with this body of repertoire for years.

The organization of the book by period is exemplary: Baroque, Classical, Romantic, and Contemporary. Also included are impressionistic literature, jazz literature, multi-period collections and anthologies, and holiday literature. An ensemble literature section (music for one piano-four hands, two pianos-four hands, and two pianos-eight hands), plus materials for adult study round out the thorough coverage. The volume is made even more useful by including suggested teaching orders plus the authors' designation of extremely successful teaching literature. The authors also grade the musical and technical difficulty of sets of pieces, i.e., Bach "Two-Part Inventions," Debussy "Préludes," etc., a big asset for young and/or inexperienced teachers.

I cannot recommend this book too highly. It is a superb contribution all piano teachers will welcome with admiration and appreciation.

Maurice Hinson, Professor of Music
The Southern Baptist Theological Seminary
Louisville, Kentucky

Preface

Due to the enthusiastic response to the first two editions of the *Intermediate Piano Repertoire Guide* and to the need to continually update our teaching repertoire, we found it necessary to undertake this third edition. This edition, which is more than double in size, includes many new and revised features:

- Summary of style characteristics for each period with suggested introductory books
- Retention of our original list with new editions included
- Expanded jazz selections
- Updated contemporary music selections
- Addition of anthologies for each period as well as a general list of multi-period collections
- Updated holiday music suggestions
- Update of our suggested teaching orders (denoted by * symbol)
- Designation of selected works which we have found to be extremely successful teaching literature (denoted by § symbol)
- Addition of one piano four-hand, two piano four-hand, and two piano eight-hand literature

We wish to thank those of you whose support, enthusiasm, and suggestions for new additions have made this revision possible. Special thanks are extended to Maurice Hinson for writing the *Foreword* to this edition and for his many helpful suggestions. We also want to acknowledge three duo-piano teams—Dallas Weekley & Nancy Arganbright, Claire Aebersohl & Ralph Neiweem, and Cristina Perotti & Laurence Lynn Dutt —who took time from their busy schedules to read and make recommendations for the ensemble portions of this edition. Personal thanks go to Frank, JoEllen, Erik and Marc for their patience and support during the completion of this project.

We have enjoyed this endeavor and hope you will find the third edition of *Intermediate Piano Repertoire: A Guide for Teaching* a useful and informative teaching reference.

Cathy Albergo   Reid Alexander

Introduction

The Intermediate level as that period of music study after the student has completed an elementary method or has mastered the concepts needed to perform elementary level repertoire. During the Intermediate level of study, the student needs to become familiar with the wide variety of musical and technical elements required to perform the "classics" of the piano repertoire. The Intermediate level is, therefore, a bridge to the more advanced repertoire such as Bach Preludes and Fugues; Haydn, Mozart, or Beethoven Sonatas; character pieces of Chopin, Schubert, or Brahms; or more advanced contemporary and jazz compositions.

In our piano pedagogy courses, we have found that students are familiar with a very narrow range of piano literature, including the compositions they currently are studying or have studied in the past, and some of the better known "standard" repertoire. They usually are not aware of the wide range of intermediate level teaching literature in each period of musical history, the wealth of materials available from lesser known composers, or the pedagogical literature of the contemporary period. This intermediate level repertoire is the stepping stone to what we think of as "standard" repertoire. To be a flexible teacher, capable of working at a variety of levels and logically preparing students for advanced repertoire, one must be familiar with this middle, intermediate range of repertoire and composers.

In the context of our own degree programs, we each teach piano practicum courses in which students are asked to observe model teaching, teach their own pupils, and prepare literature of an intermediate nature for weekly class discussion based on their own sightreading and pedagogical analysis outside of class. In this manner, students become intimately familiar with specific styles and a wide variety of piano literature. This participatory role is crucial for both graduate and undergraduate students in order that they may substantially broaden their perspectives on useful teaching editions and understand the range of difficulty within a given composer's output. Through the sightreading process, teachers and students can discover areas which may present problems for their pupils as well as identify teaching concepts within a piece.

Through our teaching of piano pedagogy and practicum courses, we continue to maintain and develop a bibliography of intermediate teaching literature, arranged by composer and style period, which we find useful as a reference tool for students as well as teachers. We feel this repertoire guide is useful in avoiding a teaching "rut," i.e., continuous use of the same pieces, and in serving as a reminder of pieces which may have been taught in the past but have since been forgotten. The guide also provides a look at lesser known or unfamiliar teaching pieces and composers. This third edition introduces many recently published editions and collections. Some advanced repertoire has been included to show the scope and range of difficulty within a given composer's writing. Much of this literature is appropriate for quite skilled high school pianists and undergraduate piano majors.

In the process of compiling this bibliography, we found an infinite number of possibilities. It is virtually impossible to be totally comprehensive. Thus, we have streamlined the list to include what we would consider the central works of any given composer, especially those works which are representative of an early intermediate to early advanced level of teaching. Editions are included as a general guide, especially for lesser known works. When more than one edition or publisher is cited, they occur in alphabetical order. Several sources were used to check availability and to obtain each composer's dates and country of birth when possible. Such data for current composers in the field are often unavailable.

Important features of *Intermediate Piano Repertoire: A Guide for Teaching* include the grading of the relative difficulty of the literature, a suggested teaching order for selected works, and the citation of works which we consider to be exceptional. Explanations of these features are as follows:

GRADING (E - I - A)

In this bibliography, we have attempted to grade the relative musical and technical difficulty of each set, realizing that there are always gray areas between and even within categories:

E (Early Intermediate)

Easy intermediate literature; entry level pieces for the particular style; a composer's easiest writing; material appropriate for introducing the classics.

I (Intermediate)

Moderately difficult pieces; possible introductory pieces to the composer's style but at least middle range difficulty within the composer's writing.

A (Advanced)

Difficult pieces that are possible for high school students, but only those who are quite skilled and highly motivated; a composer's more advanced compositions.

TEACHING ORDER (*)

For selected publications, indicated by an asterisk (*), we have given a possible teaching order and thus have grouped pieces according to a general order of difficulty, beginning with the easiest. We find that this type of categorization is helpful for pedagogy students, less experienced teachers, and those unfamiliar with a particular set of pieces. As always these are subjective opinions. They should be regarded only as general guidelines and suggestions.

Examples of this feature are as follows:

1)   Under the heading for Bach, J. S., you will find the following entry:

* Two Part Inventions (8, 1, 4, 13, 14)   Henle

The parenthetical entries suggest that a teacher might consider teaching Invention No. 8 first, then No. 1, No. 4, etc. Within this set, the entries are arranged from easiest to more difficult with No. 14 being the most difficult of those listed. Depending on the student's background, we would teach one of these five inventions first.

2)   Under the heading for Debussy, Claude, you will find the following entry:

Préludes   Durand

I-A §   *   Book I: La fille aux cheveux de lin
                                        Des pas sur la neige
                                        Minstrels
                                        Danseuses de Delphes
                                        La cathédrale engloutie

A   *   Book II: Canope
                                        Feuilles mortes
                                        La Puerta del Vino

The *préludes* most frequently taught to late intermediate and advanced students are listed in order of difficulty. We suggest introducing these works with *La fille aux cheveux de lin* or *Des pas sur la neige*. We would not, for example, teach *La cathédrale engloutie* to a late intermediate student or early advanced student as the first Debussy piece of this set.

ANNOTATED WORKS (§)

Selected editions or pieces are marked with the § symbol. These publications are among our favorite intermediate and early advanced level teaching pieces or collections. If you are looking for new literature and have not yet taught these works or used these editions, we suggest that you give them a try. Again, these are general and subjective suggestions. We could have continued labeling our favorite works, but rather, have limited the § citations to include what we consider truly exceptional or unique editions based on editorial quality and/or musical value. For anthologies, we also have included descriptive comments about each volume. In general, only books and collections are cited and not sheet music solos and duets.

Characteristic Elements

of the

Four Style Periods

	Baroque 1600 - 1750	Classical 1750 - 1820s	Romantic 1820s - 1900	Contemporary 1900 - present
Form	Prelude, Fugue Dance Suite Variations Dances Ternary Form Binary Form	Sonata Allegro Dances Variations Concerto Rondo Minuet and Trio	Character Piece Sonata Variation Concerto	Chance/Aleatoric Sonata Variation Character piece
Technic	Finger inde- pendence Contrapuntal voicing Legato, portato, staccato	Scales, arpeggios Articulation Accompaniment patterns Slurs Phrasing Balance between hands	Expansion/con- traction of hand Complex inner voicing Octave stretch, octave fill-in Balance between hands	Wide Leaps 9ths Interval fingerings: 4ths, 5ths, 7ths, etc. Legato vs. staccato accents
Rhythm	8ths, 16ths, triplets Emphasis on strong beats Emphasis on upbeat patterns	Tempo variations Rests 16ths, triplets	Syncopation Cross rhythms: 2 against 3 Complex rhythms	Shifting meter Polyrhythms
Harmony	Contrapuntal Polyphonic Frequent changes of harmony	Homophonic - stronger tonal centers Cadences Modulations 3rds Slower harmonic rhythm	Chromatic Chord doublings Dim./Dom. 7ths Secondary dominant Thick texture, full chords Accidentals	Use of 7ths, 9ths, 11ths Atonality, poly- tonality, clusters, whole tone, pen- tatonic, triadic, quartal, quintal, modal, 12 tone
Style	Ornaments Absence of phrase and expression marks Phrasing across bar line Faster notes - legato; slower notes - non legato Theme recognition and consistency	Passage work Dynamic contrasts Melody and accompaniment Phrasing and articulation Two-note slurs	Expressive - involves personal feeling Variety of phrase lengths Pedal effects Voicing Wide range of accompaniment figures Use of entire keyboard Singing lines/ cantabile Variety of dynamic and tempo markings	Prepared instruments Variety of styles, harmonies, modes, rhythms and moods Often dissonant New forms of notation More extensive and precise phrasing, dynamic and tempo markings

SOLO LITERATURE

The Baroque Period   1600 - 1750

A. Characteristics

Students entering the intermediate level of piano instruction need to prepare carefully for the demands, both musical and technical, of this literature. In order to learn and successfully perform Baroque pieces, students should be familiar with the following musical and technical elements of Baroque literature:

- Hand and finger independence
- Contrapuntal voicing; polyphonic style
- Articulation - legato, detached, and portato sounds
- Terraced dynamics
- Interpretation of phrasing (and the absence of phrase and expression markings)
- Phrasing across the bar lines
- Use of subjects, motifs, episodes, sequences, inverted motifs, etc.
  Ornamentation
- Dance forms; ternary and binary; variations; prelude and fugue; invention
- 8th, 16th, and triplet rhythms; rhythmic augmentation and diminution of melodies
- Emphasis on strong beats and on upbeat patterns

B. Music for Style Introduction

Teachers should prepare students carefully before tackling some of the more complex Baroque literature. The following is a list of music which may be used to introduce the Baroque style. These pieces and collections are examples of the type of music which can serve as a valuable link between elementary method books and more advanced repertoire. They are listed in alphabetical order by composer rather than in order of difficulty.

Bach, J. S.	Dances of J. S. Bach (Hinson ed.)	Alfred
Bach, J. S.	Kleine Präludien und Fughetten	Wiener Urtext
Bastien, James	First Piano Repertoire Album	Kjos
Collection	Easy Keyboard Music-Ancient to Modern	Alfred
Collection	Harris Piano Classics: Baroque & Classical Repertoire, Vols. 1a, 2a	Frederick Harris
Gillock, William	Fanfare & Other Courtly Scenes in Baroque Style	Summy-Birchard
Handel, G. F.	An Introduction to His Keyboard Works	Alfred
Noona, Walter ed.	Classical Performer/Patterns/Pianist A	Heritage
Olson/Bianchi/ Blickenstaff eds.	Music Pathways: Repertoire/Musicianship/ Technique 3A-3B	Fischer
Palmer, Willard	Baroque Folk	Alfred
Scarlatti, Domenico	An Introduction to His Keyboard Works	Alfred
Waxman, Donald ed.	A Dance Pageant-Renaissance & Baroque Keyboard Dances	Galaxy Music

C. Gradation

We suggest the following teaching order for Baroque literature:

Easy Dances of Bach, Handel, Purcell
Scarlatti - Easier Sonatas
Bach - Little Preludes
Bach - Two-Part Inventions
Bach - Three-Part Inventions
Bach - Well-Tempered Clavier

Baroque Literature

Composer			Title	Publisher

Bach, Johann Sebastian (1685-1750) Germany

E			An Introduction to his Keyboard Works (Palmer ed.)	Alfred
E			First Bach Album (Bastien ed.)	Kjos
E	§		The First Book for Young Pianists (Palmer ed.)	Alfred
E			First Lessons in Bach, Books 1, 2 (Carroll ed.)	Schirmer
E-I			J. S. Bach: Young Pianist's Guide to the Great Composers (Novik ed.)	Belwin
E-I			Notenbuchlein für Anna Magdalena Bach (Heinemann ed.)	Henle
E-I			Selections from the Little Clavier Book for Wilhelm Friedemann Bach (Palmer ed.)	Alfred
I			An Introduction to the Composer and His Music (Banowitz ed.)	Kjos
I			Anson Introduces Bach	Willis
I			At the Piano with J. S. Bach (Hinson ed.)	Alfred
I	§		Dances of J. S. Bach (Hinson ed.)	Alfred
I			Easiest Piano Pieces	Peters
I	§		Eighteen Short Preludes (Palmer ed.)	Alfred
I			First Lessons in Bach (Carroll/Palmer eds.)	Alfred
I	§		Inventions and Sinfonias (Palmer ed.)	Alfred
I	§	*	Kleine Präludien und Fughetten (BWV 939, 927, 924, 999, 933)	Wiener Urtext
I			Selections from The Anna Magdalena Notebook	Alfred
I			Selections from The Little Clavier Book	Alfred
I-A			An Introduction to the Performance of Bach, Vols. I-III (Tureck ed.)	Oxford
I-A			The Belwin Master Composer Series (Tucker ed.)	Belwin
I-A			The Joy of Bach	Yorktown
I-A			J. S. Bach Miscellaneous Keyboard Works	Dover
I-A			Notebook for Wilhelm Friedemann Bach	Kalmus
I-A	§	*	Two Part Inventions (8, 1, 4, 13, 14)	Henle
I-A		*	Sinfonias (1, 2, 9, 15)	Henle
A			Italian Concerto	Alfred; Henle
A			J. S. Bach Keyboard Music	Dover
A		*	Six English Suites (4)	Henle
A		*	Six French Suites (5)	Alfred; Henle
A		*	Six Partitas (1)	Alfred; Henle
A		*	The Well-Tempered Clavier: Vol. I (2, 16, 5, 21, 1)	Henle
A		*	The Well-Tempered Clavier: Vol. II (15, 1)	Henle

Blow, John (1648-1708) Great Britain

A			Six Suites	Ferguson

Bull, John (1562-1628) England

I-A			Compositions	Kalmus

Couperin, François (1668-1733) France

I-A	Album of Harpsichord Pieces	Kalmus
I-A	Couperin Complete Keyboard Works, Series I, II	Dover
I-A §	L'art de toucher le Clavecin (Halford ed.)	Alfred

Handel, George Frideric (1685-1759) England (born Germany)

E	Twelve Easy Pieces (Bulow ed.)	Kalmus
I	Allegro from Sonata in C	Summy-Birchard
I §	An Introduction to his Keyboard Works (Lucktenberg ed.)	Alfred
I	Anson Introduces Handel, Vols. I, II	Willis
I	Easier Favorites (Feldmann ed.)	Heinrichshofen
I	Easiest Piano Pieces (Pfeiffer ed.)	Peters
I	The First Book for Young Pianists (Lucktenberg ed.)	Alfred
I	Six Little Fugues	Concordia
I	The Young Pianist's Handel, Vols. I, II	Oxford
I-A	Keyboard Works for Solo Instrument	Dover
I-A	Suites, Vols. I (1-8); II (9-16)	Peters
A	Air and Variations from Suite No. 5 (Harmonious Blacksmith, Palmer ed.)	Alfred

Lugge, John (1580-1635) England

I-A	The Complete Keyboard Works (Jeans/Steele eds.)	Novello

Paradies (Paradisi), Pietro Domenico (1707-1791) Italy

I-A	Toccata (Olson ed.)	Alfred

Purcell, Henry (1659-1695) England

E-I	Eighteen Easy Piano Pieces	Peters
I	Pieces for Klavier or Harpsichord	Schott
I-A §	Keyboard Works (Squire ed.)	Dover
A	Keyboard Suites (Oesterle/Aldrich eds.)	Schirmer

Scarlatti, Domenico (1685-1757) Italy

E	The First Book for Young Pianists (Halford ed.)	Alfred
E-I §	An Introduction to his Keyboard Works (Halford ed.)	Alfred
I	At the Piano with Scarlatti (Hinson ed.)	Alfred
I-A	The Graded Scarlatti (Motchane ed.)	Belwin
I-A	Selected Sonatas (Banowetz ed.)	Kjos
I-A	Selected Sonatas (Hinson ed.)	Alfred
I-A §	Ten Sonatas (Slenczynska ed.)	Stipes
I-A	Twelve Easy Sonatas (Mirovitch ed.)	Marks
I-A	Twelve Selected Sonatas (Friskin ed.)	Belwin
A	Great Keyboard Sonatas, Vols. I, II	Dover
A	100 Sonatas in Three Volumes (Hashimoto ed.)	Kalmus
A	Piano Sonatas, Vol. II (Hinson ed.)	Alfred
A § *	Sixty Sonatas in Two Volumes (Kirkpatrick ed.)	Schirmer

Volume I (L. 378, 215, 465, 10, 204, 413)
Volume II (L. 128, 321, L.S. 2)

Soler, Antonio Padre (1729-1783) Spain

| I-A | Sonatas (complete in 7 volumes) | Unión Musical Española |

Telemann, Georg Philipp (1681-1767) Germany

I	Easy Chorale Preludes	Peters
I	Easy Fugues and Short Pieces	International
I	Little Klavier Book	Schott
I-A	The 36 Fantasias for Keyboard	Dover
A	Three Dozen Klavier Fantasias	Bärenreiter

Baroque Collections and Anthologies

A Dance Pageant - Renaissance and Baroque Keyboard Dances (Waxman ed.)	Galaxy
At the Piano With the Sons of Bach	Alfred
Bach, Handel, Scarlatti, Vols. I, II (M. Clark ed.)	Myklas
§ The Baroque Era - An Introduction to the Keyboard Music (Palmer/Halford eds.)	Alfred

(64 pages) An interesting assortment of Baroque compositions evenly divided and categorized by country.

§ Baroque Folk - Familiar Melodies arranged in Baroque Style (Palmer arr.)	Alfred

(32 pages) 16 early intermediate to intermediate level solos based on familiar melodies or folk tunes arranged in Baroque styles. Composed to prepare the student to understand and enjoy music of the Baroque period.

The Baroque Period (Agay ed.)	Yorktown
Baroque Piano (Brisman ed.)	Alfred
Byrd to Beethoven (Anthony ed.)	Presser
Early English Keyboard Music, Vols. I, II (Ferguson ed.)	Oxford
Early French Keyboard Music, Vols. I, II (Ferguson ed.)	Oxford
Early German Keyboard Music, Vols. I, II (Ferguson ed.)	Oxford
Early Italian Keyboard Music, Vols. I, II (Ferguson ed.)	Oxford
Early Keyboard Music, Vols. I, II (Oesterle ed.)	Schirmer
Easy Keyboard Music, Ancient to Modern (Palmer ed.)	Alfred
Elizabeth Rogers, Hir Virginall Booke (Cofone ed.)	Dover
English Piano Music for the Young Musician (Gyorgy ed.)	Editio Musica Budapest
Fitzwilliam Virginal Books 1, 2 (Maitland/Squire eds.)	Dover
French Piano Music for the Young Musician (Gyorgy ed.)	Editio Musica Budapest
§ Harris Piano Classics - Baroque & Classical Repertoire Volumes 1a-7a	Frederick Harris

(Volumes range from 16 to 24 pages and include 9-16 piano compositions.) Graded piano pieces include composers from all style periods. "a" volumes include Baroque and Classical repertoire.

Henry Purcell and His Contemporaries (Hermann ed.)	Hinrichsen
Introduction to Baroque Piano Literature (Schultz ed.)	Belwin
The Joy of Baroque (Agay ed.)	Yorktown
§ Masters of the Baroque Period (Hinson ed.)	Alfred

(64 pages) Wide-ranging collection of late intermediate and early advanced baroque compositions representing 14 Baroque composers.

§ Minor Masters, Vols. I-III (Clark/Goss eds.)	New School

(Each volume is 16 pages.) Compositions by lesser known composers for late elementary and early intermediate students.

The Pianist's Book of Baroque Treasures (Banowetz ed.)	Kjos
Purcell to Mozart (Anthony ed.)	Presser
Sons of Bach (Soldan ed.)	Peters

The Classical Period   1750 - 1820s

A. Characteristics

Literature of the Classical Period involves new levels of technique and musicality for the intermediate student. In order to learn and successfully perform Classical literature, students need to be familiar with the following elements of the period:

- Forms: sonata, sonata allegro, variations, dances, concerto, rondo, minuet and trio
- Scales, arpeggios, articulations such as slurs and staccatos
- Passage work, dynamic contrasts
- Melody and accompaniment; balance between the hands
- Accompaniment patterns
- 16ths, triplets, rests, tempo variations
- Cadences and modulations
- Homophonic style - stronger tonal center
- Use of rests to achieve long silences

B. Music for Style Introduction

Before beginning some of the more complex Classical literature, teachers should carefully prepare students for this level of playing. The following is a list of music which may be used to introduce the Classical style. These pieces and collections are examples of the type of music which can serve as a valuable link between elementary method books and more advanced repertoire. They are listed in alphabetical order by composer rather than in order of difficulty.

Aubry, Leon ed.	The Easiest Sonatina Album	Frederick Harris
Bastien, James ed.	First Piano Repertoire Album	Kjos
Clementi, Muzio	An Introduction to His Works (Schneider ed.)	Alfred
Clementi, Muzio	Six Progressive Sonatinas Op. 36, 6th edition (Hinson ed.)	Alfred
Collection	Harris Piano Classics: Baroque & Classical Repertoire, Vols. 1a, 2a	Frederick Harris
Czerny, Carl	Selected Piano Studies (Germer ed.)	Boston
Gillock, William	Accent on Analytical Sonatinas	Willis
Gillock, William	Sonatina in Classic Style	Willis
Noona, Walter	Classical Performer/Patterns/Pianist A	Heritage
Olson, Lynn F. ed.	Exploring Piano Literature	Fischer
Olson/Bianchi/ Blickenstaff eds.	Music Pathways: Level D Discoveries and Activities	Fischer
Olson/Bianchi/ Blickenstaff eds.	Music Pathways: Levels 3A and 3B Repertoire/Musicianship/Technique	Fischer
Olson/Hilley eds.	Essential Keyboard Sonatinas	Alfred
Palmer, Willard ed.	The First Sonatina Book	Alfred

C. Gradation

We suggest the following teaching order for intermediate Classical literature:

Easy Dances - Haydn, Beethoven, Mozart
Easy Sonatinas - Clementi, Kuhlau, Haydn, Beethoven, Mozart
Haydn - early Sonatas/Sonatinas Hob. XVI /8, 9, 10
Beethoven - Bagatelles Op. 119
Mozart - K. 545, K. 283 (Sonatas)
Beethoven - Op. 49 Nos. 2, 1 (Sonatas)

Classical Literature

Composer			Title	Publisher

Beethoven, Ludwig van (1770-1827) Germany

			Title	Publisher
E			An Introduction to his Piano Works (Palmer ed.)	Alfred
E			Anson Introduces Beethoven, Vols. I, II	Willis
E			Contra-Dances (Seiss ed.)	Schirmer
E			German Dances	Peters
E			Six Easy Variations on a Swiss Song	Summy-Birchard
E			Sixteen of His Easiest Piano Selections	Alfred
	§		Drei Variationenwerke	Henle
E			WoO 64 Variations on a Swiss Song	
I			WoO 70 Variations on "Nel cor più non mi sento"	
I			WoO 77 Six Easy Variations in G	
E-I			Beethoven: Young Pianist's Guide to the Great Composers (Novik ed.)	Belwin
I			At the Piano with Beethoven (Hinson ed.)	Alfred
I			Dances of Beethoven (Hinson ed.)	Alfred
I			Easier Favorites	Heinrichshofen
I			Für Elise (Brendel ed.)	Weiner Urtext
I			German Dances (Seiss ed.)	Schirmer
I			Rondo Op. 51 No. 1	Henle
I			7 Sonatinas (Hinson ed.)	Alfred
I		*	Sonatinas (5, 6)	Peters
I	§		Sonatina in F Major No. 2	Frederick Harris
I			13 Most Popular Piano Pieces	Alfred
I	§		Two Easy Piano Sonatas Op. 49 No. 1, Op. 49 No. 2	Henle
I	§		Two Sonatinas for Piano in F and G	Henle
I-A		*	Bagatelles Op. 119 (1, 3, 8, 11); Op. 126 (3); Op. 33 (1, 3, 4, 6)	Henle
I-A			Bagatelles Opp. 33, 119, 126 (Brendel ed.)	Weiner Urtext
I-A			Beethoven Bagatelles, Rondos, and Other Shorter Works	Dover
I-A			Beethoven: Piano Music From His Early Years (Hinson ed.)	Alfred
I-A			The Belwin Master Composer Series (Tucker ed.)	Belwin
I-A	§		Eleven Bagatelles Op. 119 (Palmer ed.)	Alfred
I-A		*	Variations, Vols. I, II (WoO 64, 69, 70, 72)	Henle
I-A			Various Pieces, Vols. I, II	Peters
I-A		*	Sonatas (Op. 49 Nos. 2, 1; Op. 2 No. 1; Op. 79; Op. 14 No. 1; Op. 10 Nos. 1, 2)	Henle
A			32 Variations in C Minor WoO 80 (Hinson ed.)	Alfred

Clementi, Muzio (1752-1832) England (born Italy)
(Keyboard player, publisher, and piano manufacturer)

			Title	Publisher
E-I	§		The First Book for Young Pianists (Schneider ed.)	Alfred
I	§		An Introduction to his Works (Schneider ed.)	Alfred
I			Eight Waltzes for Piano, Triangle and Tambourine	Schirmer
I			Preludes (from Op. 43)	Fischer
I	§		Six Progressive Sonatinas for Piano Op. 36, 6th edition (Hinson ed.)	Alfred
I			Six Sonatinas for Piano Op. 36	Frederick Harris

I		Sonatinen Opp. 36, 37, 38		Peters
	*	Six Sonatinas Op. 36 (1, 3, 2, 4)		
	*	Three Sonatinas Op. 37 (3, 2)		
	*	Three Sonatinas Op. 38 (3)		
I-A		The Belwin Master Composer Series (Tucker ed.)		Belwin
A		Gradus ad Parnassum (Tausig ed.)		Schirmer
A		Preludes and Exercises		Ricordi
A		Rediscovered Masterworks, Vols. I-III		Marks

Czerny, Carl (1791-1857) Austria

I	Selected Piano Studies, Books 1, 2 (Germer ed.)		Boston
I	Selected Piano Studies (Palmer ed.)		Alfred
I	6 Easy Sonatinas Op. 163		Cranz

Diabelli, Anton (1781-1858) Austria

I	11 Sonatinas Opp. 151, 168 (Palmer ed.)		Alfred
I-A	Selected Piano Pieces (Hinson ed.)		Alfred

Haydn, Franz Joseph (1732-1809) Austria

E			An Introduction to His Keyboard Works (Lucktenberg ed.)	Alfred
E			Anson Introduces Haydn German Dances	Willis
E			Twelve Short Piano Pieces (Palmer ed.)	Alfred
E-I			Haydn: Young Pianist's Guide to the Great Composers (Novik ed.)	Belwin
I			Arietta (Theme and Variations)	Summy-Birchard
I			At the Piano with Haydn (Hinson ed.)	Alfred
I			The First Book for Young Pianists (Lucktenberg ed.)	Alfred
I	§	*	Six Sonatinas (the early sonatas) (Hob. XVI/8, 4, 11, 7, 9, 10)	Alfred
I-A			Sonatas (complete)	Wiener Urtext
I	§	*	Band 1a (Hob. XVI/8, 9, 10)	
A		*	Band 1b (Hob. XVI/43)	
A		*	Band 2 (Hob. XVI/23, 35, 37)	
A		*	Band 3 (Hob. XVI/34, 49, 50, 51)	
A			Oxford Keyboard Classics—Haydn (Ferguson ed.)	Oxford
A			Piano Sonatas (complete), Vols. I, II	Dover
A			Sonatas (complete), Vols. I-III (Hinson ed.)	Alfred

Kuhlau, (Daniel) Friedrich (Rudolph) (1786-1832) Denmark (born Germany)

I	*	Sonatinas, Books 1, 2 (Klee ed.)	Schirmer
		(Op. 55 Nos. 1, 2, 3; Op. 20 Nos. 1, 2, 3; Op. 88 No. 3)	
I	*	Sonatinas, Vols. I, II (Op. 88 Nos. 3, 2, 1, 4; Op. 60 No. 1)	Kalmus
I		Sonatinen, Band I	Peters

Mozart, (Johann Chrysostom) Wolfgang Amadeus (1756-1791) Austria

E	§	The First Book for Young Pianists (Palmer ed.)	Alfred
E-I		Mozart: Piano Music from His Early Years (Hinson ed.)	Alfred
E-I		Mozart: Young Pianist's Guide to the Great Composers (Novik ed.)	Belwin
I		An Introduction to his Keyboard Works (Palmer ed.)	Alfred
I		At the Piano with Mozart (Hinson ed.)	Alfred
I		The Easiest Original Pieces for Piano	Hinrichsen

I		German Dances	Peters
I		Klavierstücke	Henle
I		Mozart, Easier Favorites (Feldmann ed.)	Heinrichshofen
I		Selected Piano Pieces	Peters
I	*	Six Viennese Sonatinas (1, 5, 4, 6) (Rehberg ed.)	Schott
I		The Young Mozart	Schott
I-A		Piano Pieces	Peters
I-A §	*	Sonatas and Fantasies (K. 545, 283, 282, 332; Fantasia in D Minor, K. 397)	Presser
I-A		Variations (Ah, vous dirai-je, Maman) (Hinson ed.)	Alfred
I-A		Variations (Ah, vous dirai-je, Maman)	Henle

Reinagle, Alexander (1756-1809)

E	24 Short and Easy Pieces (Hinson/Krauss eds.)	Alfred

Türk, Daniel Gottlob (1750-1813) Germany

E	Easy Pieces for Piano	Schott
E	Little Piece	Nagel
E	Sixty Pieces for the Beginner	Litolff

Classical Collections and Anthologies

	The Classical Era (Palmer/Halford eds.)	Alfred
	Classical Piano (Brisman ed.)	Alfred
	The Classical Period, Vol. II (Agay ed.)	Yorktown
	Das neue Sonatinen Buch, I, II (Frey ed.)	Schott
§	The Days of Haydn, Mozart, and Beethoven (Wier ed.)	Belwin Mills

(192 pages) Features intermediate piano compositions by lesser known composers such as Cherubini, Cimarosa, Stamitz and Steibelt.

	Early Classical Sonatas, Vols. I, II (Smart ed.)	Schirmer
	Early English Sonatinas (Rowley ed.)	Boosey & Hawkes
	First Sonatinas (Bastien ed.)	Kjos
	First Sonatina Album (Bastien ed.)	Kjos
	The First Sonatina Book (Palmer ed.)	Alfred
§	Harris Piano Classics - Baroque & Classical Repertoire Volumes 1a-7a	Frederick Harris

(Volumes range from 16 to 24 pages and include 9-16 piano compositions.) Graded piano pieces include composers from all style periods. "a" volumes include Baroque and Classical repertoire.

	Introduction to Classical Piano Literature (Schultz ed.)	Belwin
	Introduction to Theme & Variations (Halford ed.)	Alfred
	The Joy of Sonatinas (Agay ed.)	Yorktown
§	Minor Masters, Vols. I-III (Clark/Goss eds.)	New School

(Each volume is 16 pages.) Compositions by lesser known composers for late elementary and early intermediate students.

	Masters of the Classical Period (Hinson ed.)	Alfred
	Masters of the Sonatina, Vols. I-III (Hinson ed.)	Alfred
	The Pianist's Book of Classic Treasures (Banowetz ed.)	Kjos
	Selected Sonatinas, Vols. I-III	Schirmer
	Sonatina Album (Kohler ed.)	Schirmer
§	Sonatina Album (Small ed.)	Alfred

(144 pages) This newly engraved version of the Sonatina Album, *a favorite of many teachers, includes newly revised fingerings by the editor and additional sonatinas by Beethoven and Diabelli. Other works include Clementi (all sonatinas from Opus 36), Dussek, Haydn, Kuhlau (Opus 20 and Opus 55 sonatinas), and Mozart's Sonata in C Major K. 545. The spiral binding permits the book to lie flat.*

	Sonatina Favorites, Vols. I-III (Bastien ed.)	Kjos
	Sonatinas (varied styles and levels), Vols. I, II (M. Clark ed.)	Myklas
	Sonatinas for Piano, Vol. II, Classic Era (Herttrich/Kraus eds.)	Henle
	Sonatinen Album, Vol. I (Kohler/Ruthardt eds.)	Peters
	Sonatinen für Klavier, Vols. I, II	Henle
	Style and Interpretation, Vol. III (Ferguson ed.)	Oxford
	World's Greatest Classical Sonatas, Vols. I, II (Hinson ed.)	Alfred

The Romantic Period   circa 1820 - 1900

A. Characteristics

Literature of the Romantic Period requires more complex technical demands. Students entering the intermediate level of piano instruction need to prepare carefully for the new demands—both musical and technical—this literature brings. In order to learn Romantic literature, students need to be familiar with and ready to handle the following musical elements of the Romantic period:

- Character and descriptive pieces, concerto, variations, sonata
- Expansion and contraction of the hand, complex inner voicing, finger
    independence, octave stretch and octave fill-in
- Balance between hands and within the hand
- Voicing of melodic lines
- Wide range of accompaniment figures
- Use of entire keyboard
- Singing lines, *cantabile*
- Sudden dynamic changes; variety of phrase lengths
- Expressive qualities
- Syncopation, complex rhythms, cross rhythms
- Variety of tempo markings
- Chromatic harmonies, thick textures, chord doublings
- Secondary dominants, diminished 7ths, modulations
- Accidentals
- Pedaling

B. Music for Style Introduction

Teachers should prepare students carefully before beginning more complex Romantic repertoire. The following is a list of music which may be used to introduce the Romantic style. These pieces and collections are examples of literature which can serve as a valuable link between elementary method books and more advanced repertoire. They are listed in alphabetical order by composer rather than in order of difficulty.

Bürgmuller, Johann	25 Progressive Pieces Op. 100	Alfred
Collection	Harris Piano Classics: Vols. 1b & 2b	Frederick Harris
	Romantic & 20th-century Repertoire	
Gillock, William	Lyric Preludes in Romantic Style	Summy-Birchard
Grieg, Edvard	The First Book for Young Pianists (Halford ed.)	Alfred
Gurlitt, Cornelius	I Remember Gurlitt (F. Clark ed.)	New School
Heller, Stephen	Fifty Selected Studies	Schirmer
Olson, Lynn F.	Adventures in Style	Fischer
Rocherolle, Eugenie	Six Moods for Piano	Kjos
Rollin, Catherine	Preludes for Piano (Vol. I)	Alfred
Schumann, Robert	Album for the Young Op. 68	Alfred
Sheftel, Paul	Patterns for Fun (Vols. I, II)	Douglas
Tchaikovsky, Pyotr	Album for the Young Op. 39	Alfred
Vandall, Robert	Preludes (Vol. I)	Myklas

C. Gradation

To introduce Romantic literature, we suggest the following order:

Gurlitt - easy pieces
Bürgmuller Etudes
Heller Etudes
Schumann - Album for the Young
Tchaikovsky - Album for the Young
Grieg - Lyric Pieces
Mendelssohn - Songs Without Words
Chopin - easier Preludes and Mazurkas

Romantic Literature

Composer	Title	Publisher

Berens, J. Hermann (1826-1880) Germany

I	Twenty Children's Studies Op. 79	Schirmer

Brahms, Johannes (1833-1897) Germany

I-A		At the Piano with Brahms (Hinson ed.)	Alfred
I-A		The Belwin Master Composer Series (Tucker ed.)	Belwin
I-A		Complete Shorter Works (Mandyczewski ed.)	Dover
I-A §		Dances of Brahms (Hinson ed.)	Alfred
I-A §	*	Waltzes Op. 39 (3, 5, 9, 15, 1)	Henle
I-A		The Young Pianist's Brahms (Dexter ed.)	Hansen
A		Ballades Op. 10 (Hinson ed.)	Alfred
A		Complete Sonatas & Variations (Mandyczewski ed.)	Dover
A	*	Eight Piano Pieces Op. 76 (2)	Henle
A	*	Four Ballades Op. 10 (1)	Henle
A	*	Four Piano Pieces Op. 119 (3)	Henle
A		Intermezzi Op. 117 (Palmer ed.)	Alfred
A		Sarabandes and Gigues	Peters
A	*	Seven Fantasies Op. 116 (3, 6)	Henle
A		The Shorter Piano Pieces (Hinson ed.)	Alfred
A	*	Six Piano Pieces Op. 118 (1, 2)	Henle
A	*	Two Rhapsodies Op. 79 (2)	Henle

Bruckner, (Joseph) Anton (1824-1896) Austria

I-A	Werke (complete)	Musikwissenschaftlicher Verlag Wien

Bürgmuller, Johann F. (1806-1874) Germany

I	§	25 Progressive Pieces Op. 100 (Palmer ed.)	Alfred
I-A		18 Characteristic Studies Op. 109 (Hinson ed.)	Alfred
A		12 Brilliant and Melodious Studies (Hinson ed.)	Alfred

Chopin, Frédéric François (1810-1849) Poland
(Fryderyk Franciszek)

E	§	The First Book for Young Pianists (Palmer ed.)	Alfred
E-I	§	An Introduction to his Piano Works (includes posthumous Waltz in A Minor) (Palmer ed.)	Alfred
E-I		Chopin: Young Pianist's Guide to the Great Composers (Novik ed.)	Belwin
E-I	§	Selected Easy Pieces	Chopin Institute
I-A		The Belwin Master Composer Series (Tucker ed.)	Belwin
I-A		Chopin: Piano Music from His Early Years (Hinson ed.)	Alfred
I-A		Dances of Chopin (Hinson ed.)	Alfred
I-A		Frédéric Chopin Piano Compositions (Tucker ed.)	Belwin
I-A	*	Mazurkas (Op. 68 No. 3; Op. 7 Nos. 1, 2; Op. 17 No. 2; Op. 33 No. 2)	Chopin Institute
I-A	*	Preludes (Op. 28 Nos. 4, 6, 7, 9, 15, 20, 22)	Chopin Institute
I-A		Selected Favorites (Palmer ed.)	Alfred

I-A	*		Waltzes (Op. 69 Nos. 1, 2; Op. 34 No. 2; Op. 64 Nos. 1, 2; Op. 70 No. 2)	Chopin Institute
A			At the Piano with Chopin (Hinson ed.)	Alfred
A	*		Etudes (Op. 10 Nos. 3, 6, 9; Op. 25 Nos. 1, 2, 7)	Chopin Institute
A			Fantaisie-Impromptu (Hinson ed.)	Alfred
A	*		Nocturnes (Op. 9 No. 2; Op. 15 No. 3; Op. 72 No. 1; Op. 37 No. 1)	Chopin Institute
A	*		Polonaises (Op. 26 No. 1; Op. 40 No. 1; Op. 32 No. 1; Op. 55 No. 1)	Chopin Institute
A	§		Prelude in C Major Op. 28 No. 1 (Slenczynska ed.)	Kjos
A	§		Prelude in C-sharp Minor Op. 28 No. 10 (Slenczynska ed.)	Kjos
A	§		Prelude in E Major Op. 28 No. 9 (Slenczynska ed.)	Kjos
A	§		Prelude in G Minor Op. 28 No. 22 (Slenczynska ed.)	Kjos

Elmenreich, Albert (1816-1905) Germany

E		Spinning Song Op. 14 No. 4	Schirmer

Fauré, Gabriel (Urbain) (1845-1924) France

I-A		Berceuse Op. 56 No. 1	Hamelle
I-A		Complete Préludes, Impromptus, and Valses-Caprices	Dover
I-A		13 Nocturnes	International
I-A		Selected Works	Kalmus
A		Fauré: Album of Piano Pieces (Philipp ed.)	Schirmer
A		Impromptu No. 2 in F Minor Op. 31	International
A	*	Six Barcarolles (4)	Kalmus

Field, John (1782-1837) Ireland

I-A		Selected Piano Works	Fischer
A	*	Eighteen Nocturnes (B-flat Major)	Peters

Franck, César (-Auguste-Jean-Guillaume-Hubert) (1822-1890) France (born Belgium)

I		46 Short Pieces for Piano (Agay ed.)	Presser
I		7 Traditional French Noëls	Werner-Curwen
I		18 Short Pieces	Peters
I-A		Selected Piano Compositions (d'Indy ed.)	Dover
A		Prélude, Chorale et Fugue	Peters

Gottschalk, Louis Moreau (1829-1869) U.S.A.

I-A		Album	Kalmus
A		Piano Music of Louis Moreau Gottschalk (Jackson ed.)	Dover

Grieg, Edvard (Hagerup) (1843-1907) Norway

E-I			First Book for Young Pianists (Halford ed.)	Alfred
I	§		An Introduction to his Piano Works (Halford ed.)	Alfred
I			Poetic Tone Pictures Op. 3	Peters
I-A			Grieg, Easier Favorites (Feldmann ed.)	Peters
I-A			Norwegian Dances and Songs Op. 17	Peters
	§	*	Lyric Pieces	Peters
I			Op. 12 (Waltz, National Song, Arietta, Elfin Dance)	
I-A			Op. 38 (Norwegian Dance)	
I-A			Op. 43 (To the Spring)	

I-A			Op. 47 (Norwegian Dance)	
I-A			Op. 54 (March of the Dwarfs, Notturno)	
I-A			Op. 57 (Illusion)	
I-A			Op. 62 (Home-ward)	
I-A			Op. 65 (Peasant's Song, Wedding-Day at Troldhaugen)	
I-A			Op. 68 (Sailor's Song)	
I-A			Op. 71 (Puck)	
I-A			Lyric Pieces for Piano (complete)	Dover
I-A			Lyric Pieces Opp. 12, 38 (Hinson ed.)	Alfred
I-A			Selected Works for the Piano (Levine ed.)	Alfred
A			Norwegian Dances and Other Works for Piano	Dover

Gurlitt, Cornelius (1820-1901) Germany

E	§		I Remember Gurlitt, Vols. I, II (F. Clark ed.)	New School
E			First Lessons Op. 117	Kalmus
E-I			Der Neue Gurlitt, Vols. I, II	Schott
I		*	Album for the Young Op. 140 (20 pieces) (Nos. 15, 3) (Palmer ed.)	Alfred
I			Album Leaves for the Young Op. 101	Schirmer
I			6 Sonatinas Op. 54 (Palmer ed.)	Alfred

Heller, Stephen (1813-1888) Frznce (born Hungary)

I	§	*	Fifty Selected Studies from Opp. 45, 46, 47 (3, 6, 13, 16) (Oesterle ed.)	Schirmer
I-A			Album for the Young Op. 138	Kalmus
I-A			Melodious Studies Complete (Palmer ed.)	Alfred
I-A			Selected Progressive Etudes (Olson ed.)	Alfred
A			Warriors' Song Op. 45 No. 15	Schirmer

Liszt, Franz (1811-1886) Hungary

I-A		An Introduction to the Composer and his Music (Banowetz ed.)	Kjos
I-A §		At the Piano with Liszt (Hinson ed.)	Alfred
I-A §		Liszt: Forgotten Masterpieces (Banowetz ed.)	Kjos
I-A		Liszt: Piano Music from His Early Years (Hinson ed.)	Alfred
A		Christmas Tree, Vols. I, II	Peters
A		Hungarian Rhapsodie No. 2 (Bendel ed.)	Schirmer
A		Six Consolations (Hinson ed.)	Alfred
A		Three Liebesträume	Peters

MacDowell, Edward (Alexander) (1861-1908) U.S.A.

I			Eight Sea Pieces Op. 55	Elkan-Vogel
I			Six Fireside Tales Op. 61	Alfred
I			Forgotten Fairy Tales Op. 4 (Hinson ed.)	Alfred
I			Scotch Poem Op. 31 No. 2	Schirmer
I			Six Fancies Op. 7	Alfred
I	§	*	Ten Woodland Sketches Op. 51 (To A Wild Rose)	Schirmer
I-A			Piano Works	Dover
A			Praeludium (First Modern Suite)	Shawnee
A		*	Twelve Studies Op. 39 (Alla Tarantella, Hungarian, Shadow Dance, Romanze)	Boston
A			Two Fantastic Dances Op. 17	Presser

Mendelssohn (-Bartholdy), (Jakob Ludwig) Felix (1809-1847) Germany

I-A §	*	Songs Without Words (Hinson ed.)		Alfred
I			Op. 30 No. 3 Consolation	
I			Op. 62 No. 4 Morning Song	
I			Op. 85 No. 1 Reverie	
I			Op. 102 No. 6 Faith	
I			Op. 19 No. 6 Venetian Boat Song No. 1	
I			Op. 30 No. 6 Venetian Boat Song No. 2	
A			Op. 102 No. 3 Tarantella	
I-A §		At the Piano with Felix and Fanny Mendelssohn (Hinson ed.)		Alfred
I-A		Six Children's Pieces Op. 72 (Christmas Pieces)		Peters
I-A		Works for Piano Solo (complete), Vols. I, II		Dover
A		Fantasy-Scherzo in E Minor Op. 16 No. 2		Editio Musica Budapest
A		Rondo Capriccioso Op. 14 (Klauser ed.)		Schirmer
A		Variations Sérieuses Op. 54		Peters

Moszkowski, Moritz (1854-1925) Germany

I	Étincelles Op. 36 No. 6	Schirmer
I	Spanish Dances Op. 12	Peters

Pischna [Pišna], Josef (1826-1896) Bohemia

E-I	60 Progressive Studies	Kalmus
E-I	The Little Pischna	Kalmus

Rachmaninoff, Sergey (1873-1943) Russia
(Rakhmaninov, Sergey; born Semyonov, Russia; died Beverly Hills)

I-A §	*	Album of Piano Works (Four Improvisations, easiest of earlier compositions)	Alfred
A		Etude Op. 39 No. 2	Boosey & Hawkes
A		Humoreske Op. 10 No. 5 (Oesterle ed.)	Schirmer
A		Prelude in C-sharp Minor Op. 3 No. 2 (Oesterle ed.)	Schirmer
A		Polichinelle Op. 3 No. 4 (Oesterle ed.)	Schirmer
A	*	Ten Preludes Op. 23 (5, 10)	Boosey & Hawkes
A	*	Thirteen Preludes Op. 32 (5, 7, 10, 12)	Boosey & Hawkes

Respighi, Ottorino (1879-1936) Italy

I	Notturno	Schirmer

Schubert, Franz (Peter) (1797-1828) Austria

I	§	Dances of Schubert (Hinson ed.)	Alfred
I-A		An Introduction to his Works (Halford ed.)	Alfred
I-A	*	Dances, Vols. I, II (D 844, 841, 681, 421)	Henle
I-A		Dances for Piano (Zeitlin ed.)	Presser
I-A		Dances for Piano	Dover
A		Complete Sonatas (Epstein ed.)	Dover
A	*	Four Impromptus Op. 90 (3, 2, 4)	Henle
A	*	Four Impromptus Op. 142 (2, 3)	Henle
A	§	Impromptu in A-flat Major Op. 142 No. 2	Frederick Harris
A	§	Moments Musicaux and Impromptus Opp. 90, 94, 142 (Baylor ed.)	Alfred

| A | | | Shorter Works | Dover |
| A | | * | Six Moments Musicaux Op. 94 (2, 3) | Henle |

Schumann, Robert (Alexander) (1810-1856) Germany

E			The First Book for Young Pianists (Palmer ed.)	Alfred
E-I			Album for the Young and Scenes from Childhood (Banowetz ed.)	Kjos
E-I	§	*	Album for the Young Op. 68 (Palmer ed.)	Alfred
			(Melody, Chorale, Soldier's March, Wild Horseman,	
			Little Etude, First Loss, Knecht Ruprecht)	
E-I			An Introduction to his Piano Works (Palmer ed.)	Alfred
E-I			Schumann: Young Pianist's Guide to the Great Composers (Novik ed.)	Belwin
I		*	Album-Leaves Op. 124 (Fantastic Dance)	Peters
I	§		An Introduction to his Piano Works (Palmer ed.)	Alfred
I			Arabesque Op. 18	Henle
I			Colored Leaves Op. 99	Henle
I		*	Forest Scenes Op. 82 (The Prophetic Bird, Hunting Song)	Henle
I	§	*	Kinderszenen Op. 15	Peters
			(About Strange Lands and People, Important Event, Frightening,	
			The Poet Speaks, Reverie)	
I		*	Three Romances Op. 28 (2)	Peters
I	§	*	Unpublished Pieces from Album for the Young Op. 68	Belwin
			(Wild Horseman, Playing Tag, Preludio, Cuckoo)	
I-A			An Introduction to the Composer and his Music	Kjos
I-A			At the Piano with Robert and Clara Schumann (Hinson ed.)	Alfred
I-A			Piano Music of Robert Schumann, Series I, II, III	Dover
I-A			29 Most Popular Pieces (Palmer ed.)	Alfred
A	§	*	Fantasiestücke Op. 12 (Warum, Grillen, Aufschwung)	Henle
A			Papillons (Hinson ed.)	Alfred
A			Schumann, Easier Favorites (Feldmann ed.)	Peters
A			3 Kleine Klavierstücke	Doblinger

Sinding, Christian (August) (1856-1941) Norway

| I | | | Rustles of Spring Op. 32 No. 3 (Hinson ed.) | Alfred |

Tchaikovsky, Pyotr Il'yich (1840-1893) Russia

E-I			Easiest Piano Pieces from Album for the Young (Niemann ed.)	Peters
E-I	§	*	Tchaikovsky: Album for the Young Op. 39 (Novik ed.)	Alfred
			(French Song, Dolly's Funeral, Mazurka)	
I			Humoresque in G Major Op. 10 No. 2	Schirmer
I-A			At the Piano with Tchaikovsky (Hinson ed.)	Alfred
A			Chanson Triste in G Minor Op. 40 No. 2	Schirmer
A			Tschaikowsky Album	Editio Musica Budapest

Romantic Collections and Anthologies

	Contemporaries of Schumann (Hermann ed.)	Hinrichsen
	Early Romantic Treasures (Banowetz ed.)	Kjos
§	Harris Piano Classics - Romantic & 20th Century Repertoire	Frederick Harris

(Volumes 1b-7b range from 16 to 24 pages and include 9-12 piano compositions each.)
Graded piano pieces include composers from both style periods. "b" volumes contain
Romantic and 20th-century repertoire.

	Late Romantic Treasures (Banowetz ed.)	Kjos
	Masters of the Romantic Period (Hinson ed.)	Alfred
	Nineteenth-Century American Piano Music (Gillespie ed.)	Dover
	Nineteenth-Century European Piano Music (Gillespie ed.)	Dover
	The Pianist's Book of Early Romantic Treasures (Banowetz ed.)	Kjos
	The Pianist's Book of Late Romantic Treasures (Banowetz ed.)	Kjos
§	Piano Music in 19th Century America, Vols. I, II (Hinson ed.)	Alfred
	Play Romantic Germany	Faber
	Play Romantic Italy	Faber
	Play Romantic Paris	Faber
	Play Romantic Russia	Faber
	Play Romantic Vienna	Faber
§	Rare Masterpieces of Russian Piano Music (Feofanov ed.)	Dover

(130 pages) Eleven pieces by composers such as Glinka, Balakirev, and Glazunov.
Difficulty levels range from late intermediate to advanced.

	The Romantic Era (Palmer/Halford eds.)	Alfred
§	Romantic Masters (Kobler ed.)	Peters

(32 pages) 24 early intermediate pieces by nine 19th-century composers such as
Schubert, Chopin, Smetana, Brahms, and Grieg.

	The Romantic Period, Vol. III (Agay ed.)	Yorktown
	The Romantic Pianist, Vols. I-IV (Johnson ed.)	Peters
	The Russian Romantics	Schirmer
	Schubert to Shostakovich (Anthony ed.)	Presser
	Style and Interpretation, Vol. IV (Ferguson ed.)	Oxford
	The Joy of Romantic Piano, Vols. I, II (Agay ed.)	Yorktown

The Contemporary Period

Impressionism   1890-1920

A. Characteristics

In order to learn Impressionistic literature, students need to be familiar with and ready to handle the following musical characteristics of the Impressionistic period:

-Imagery
-Pedal effects
-Layering of sounds
-Pentatonic, whole tone colors
-Expressive and evocative writing
-Character piece
-Use of 7ths, 9ths, 11ths, 13ths
-Use of quartal and quintal chords

B. Music for Style Introduction

The following is a list of music which may be used to introduce the Impressionistic style. These pieces and collections are examples of literature which can serve as a valuable link between elementary method books and more advanced repertoire of this period. They are listed in alphabetical order by composer rather than in order of difficulty.

Bloch, Ernest	Enfantines	Fischer
Debussy, Claude	Le petit nègre	Alfred
Ibert, Jacques	Histoires	Alphonse Leduc
Rebikov, Vladimir	Silhouettes Op. 31	Alfred
Satie, Eric	Three Gymnopédies	Kalmus
Sheftel, Paul	Interludes	Fischer

C. Gradation

We recommend the following order for introducing the music of Debussy:

- The Little Shepherd from Children's Corner
- Le petit nègre
- La fille aux cheveux de lin (Préludes, Book 1)
- Des pas sur la neige (Préludes, Book 1)
- Canope (Préludes, Book 2)
- First Arabesque

Impressionistic Literature

Composer			Title	Publisher
Bloch, Ernest (1880-1959) U.S.A. (born Switzerland)				
E-I	§	*	Enfantines, Ten Pieces for Children (Lullaby, Elves, Dream)	Fischer
I			Poems of the Sea	Schirmer
A			In the Night	Schirmer
Debussy, (Achille-) Claude (1862-1918) France				
I	§	*	Children's Corner (The Little Shepherd, Doctor	Durand
			Gradus ad Parnassum, Golliwog's Cake-Walk)	
I			Danse	Durand
I	§		Le petit nègre	Alfred
I			Page d'album	Presser
I			Rêverie	Peters
I			Two Arabesques	Durand
I-A			An Introduction to His Piano Music (Halford ed.)	Alfred
I-A			The Belwin Master Composer Series (Tucker ed.)	Belwin
I-A			Dances of Debussy (Hinson ed.)	Alfred
I-A			Etudes, Children's Corner, Images Book 2, Other Works	Dover
I-A	§		Piano Music (1888-1905)	Dover
I-A			Selected Favorites (Olson ed.)	Alfred
I-A	§	*	Préludes, Vols. I, II (Hinson ed.)	Alfred; Durand
			Book I: La fille aux cheveux de lin	
			Des pas sur la neige	
			Minstrels	
			Danseuses de Delphes	
			La cathédrale engloutie	
	§	*	Book II: Canope	
			Feuilles mortes	
			La Puerta del Vino	
A	§		At the Piano with Debussy (Hinson ed.)	Alfred
A			Debussy Selected Favorites (Olson ed.)	Alfred
A		*	Estampes (Jardins sous la pluie)	Durand
A			The Joy of Claude Debussy (Agay ed.)	Yorktown
A			Pour le Piano (Hinson ed.)	Alfred
A		*	Suite Bergamasque (Prélude, Clair de lune)	Peters
A		*	Suite Pour le Piano (Sarabande)	Durand
Griffes, Charles Tomlinson (1884-1920) U.S.A.				
A		*	Four Roman Sketches Op. 7 (The White Peacock, The Fountain of Acqua Paolo)	Schirmer
A			Three Preludes	Peters
A		*	Three Tone Poems Op. 5 (Night Winds)	Schirmer
Ibert, Jacques (1890-1962) France				
I-A	§	*	Histoires (Le petit âne blanc, A giddy girl)	Alphonse Leduc
I-A			Petite Suite en Quinze Images	Foetisch

Ravel, Joseph Maurice (1875-1937) France

I-A	§		At the Piano with Ravel (Hinson ed.)	Alfred
I-A			Pavane pour une Infante défunte (1899)	Schirmer
I-A	§		Valses Nobles et Sentimentales (1911)	Durand
A			Menuet antique (1895)	Marks
A			Menuet sur le nom de Haydn (1909)	Durand
A			Piano Masterpieces	Dover
A	§	*	Sonatine (I) (1905)	Durand

Rebikov, Vladimir Ivanovich (1866-1920) Russia

E		Anson Introduces Rebikoff	Willis
E		Pictures for Children Op. 37 (Gretchaninoff ed.)	International
I	§	Nine Silhouettes Op. 31 (Palmer ed.)	Alfred

Satie, Eric (Alfred Leslie) (1866-1925) France

E		Menus Propos Enfantines (1913) (3 sets of children's pieces)	ESC
E-I	§	3 Gymnopédies (1888) and 3 Gnossiennes (1890) (Baylor ed.)	Alfred
I		Trois Gymnopédies (1888)	Salabert
I-A		Gymnopédies, Gnossiennes and Other Works for Piano	Dover
I-A		Sports et Divertissements (1914) (20 Brief Sketches)	Dover

The Twentieth Century   1900 - Present

A. Characteristics

In order to learn Contemporary literature, students need to be familiar with the following musical characteristics of the Contemporary period:

- Character piece, sonata, variation
- Chance pieces (aleatoric)
- Shifting meters, polyrhythms
- Wide leaps
- Interval fingerings - 4ths, 5ths, 7ths, etc.
- Legato vs staccato accents
- Harmonic extensions - 7ths, 9ths, 11ths
- Atonality; polytonality; 12 tone composition
- Clusters, whole tone, pentatonic, triadic, quartal, quintal, modal harmonies
- New forms of notation
- More extensive interpretation markings
- Prepared instruments
- Use of dissonance
- More extensive and precise phrase, dynamic, and tempo markings

B. Music for Style Introduction

The following is a list of music which may be used to introduce the Contemporary style. These pieces and collections are examples of literature which can serve as a valuable link between elementary method books and more advanced repertoire. They are listed in alphabetical order by composer rather than in order of difficulty.

Barratt, Carol	Play It Again, Chester, Vol. I	Chester
Bartók, Béla	For Children, Vol. I	Boosey & Hawkes
Caramia, Tony	Folksongs Revisited	New School
Collection	Contemporary Piano Literature	Summy-Birchard
Collection	Harris Piano Classics-Romantic and 20th-century Repertoire, Vols. 1b, 2b	Frederick Harris
Collection	Supplementary Solos, Book 1	Summy-Birchard
Colley, Betty	Styles for Piano	Kjos
Dello Joio, Norman	Suite for the Young	Schirmer
George, Jon	Kaleidoscope Solos, Book 3	Alfred
Finney, Ross Lee	Games (32 short pieces)	Peters
Kabalevsky, Dmitri	30 Piano Pieces Op. 27 (Palmer ed.)	Alfred
Khachaturian, Aram	Adventures of Ivan	MCA
Miller, Marguerite ed.	Mosaics	Sonos
Pearce, Elvina	Sound Reflections, Vol. I	Alfred
Pinto, Octavio	Scenas Infantis	Schirmer
Previn, André	Impressions for Piano	Leeds
Rocherolle, Eugenie	Six Moods for Piano	Kjos
Rubinstein, Beryl	A Day in the Country	Fischer
Sheftel, Paul	Patterns for Fun	Alfred
Starer, Robert	Sketches in Color	MCA
Vandall, Robert	Daydream	Myklas
Vandall, Robert	Preludes, Vol. I	Myklas

C. Gradation

Although there is so much Contemporary literature that it is difficult to limit suggestions to only a few pieces, we suggest the following teaching order of selected intermediate level Contemporary literature:

- Easy Bartók and Kabalevsky pieces
- Khachaturian - Adventures of Ivan
- Satie - Gymnopédies
- Dello Joio - Suite for the Young
- Bartók - Rumanian Folk Dances
- Persichetti - Parades Op. 57
- Labunski - Four Variations on a Theme by Paginini
- Prokofiev - Music for Children Op. 65
- Tcherepnin - Bagatelles
- Bartók - Suite Op. 14
- Gershwin - Preludes

Twentieth Century Literature (Includes Jazz Selections)

Composer		Title	Publisher

Adler, Samuel (born 1928) U.S.A. (born Germany)

E-I		Gradus 60 Studies, Vols. I, II, III	Oxford

Agay, Denes (born 1911) U.S.A. (born Hungary)

E	§	Fifteen Little Pieces On Five Note Patterns	Boston
E		Nine Easy Miniatures	Sam Fox
I		Concertina Barocco on Themes by Handel	Schirmer
I		Dance Scherzo	Schirmer
I		Four Dance Impressions	Presser
I		Petit Trianon Suite (10 easy pieces)	Schirmer
I		Sonatina Toccata	Boosey & Hawkes
I		Sonatina Hungarica	MCA
I		3 Recital Dances (Parade Polka, Waltz Serenade, Mardi Gras Bolero)	Presser
I-A		Mosaics	MCA

Alcon, Susan (born 1953) U.S.A.

I		Strolling Along	Frederick Harris

Alexander, Dennis (U.S.A.)

E-I		Just for You, Vols. I-III	Alfred
I	§	A Splash of Color, Vols. I, II	Alfred
I		Performing in Style	Alfred
I-A		Planet Earth	Alfred
I-A		Simply Sensational, Vols. I, II	Alfred

Altman, Lawrence (U.S.A.)

E		Piano Poems	Presser

Archer, Violet (born 1913) Canada

I		Eleven Short Pieces	Peer International
I-A		Sonatina No. 2	Boosey & Hawkes

Baker, Martha and Jack Reidling (U.S.A.)

E-I		Jazz Designs from the Blues	MESA Press

Barber, Samuel (1910-1981) U.S.A.

A	*	Excursions Op. 20 (2, 4)	Schirmer
A	§	Nocturne	Schirmer

Barratt, Carol (U.S.A.)

E			Play It Again, Chester, Vols. 1, 2	Chester

Bartók, Béla (1881-1945) Hungary

E			Fifteen Hungarian Peasant Songs and Dances	Universal
E			Ten Easy Piano Pieces	MCA
E			The First Term (at the Piano) (1911)	Kalmus
E-I			For Children, Vols. I, II	Boosey & Hawkes/Schirmer
E-I			Young People at the Piano, Vols. I, II	Boosey & Hawkes
E-A			Mikrokosmos (6 volumes)	Boosey & Hawkes
I	§		An Introduction to his Piano Works (Palmer ed.)	Alfred
I			The Joy of Bartók (Agay ed.)	Yorktown
I	§	*	Six Rumanian Folk Dances (2, 4, 1, 3)	Boosey & Hawkes
I	§		Sonatina	Schirmer
I			Three Hungarian Folk Songs	Boosey & Hawkes
I			Three Rondos on Folk Tunes	Boosey & Hawkes
I-A		*	Fourteen Bagatelles Op. 6 (1, 3, 4, 6)	Kalmus
I-A			Piano Music of Béla Bartók, Series I, II	Dover
A			Allegro Barbaro	Universal
A			Selected Works	Schirmer
A	§		Suite Op. 14	Universal

Beard, Katherine (U.S.A.)

I	Echoes of America, Books 1, 2	Willis

Beattie, Donald (U.S.A.)

E	Three Easy Pieces (The Earth, Autumn, The Sea)	HAS

Beaty, Dan (U.S.A.)

I	Woodsprite and Waterbug	Kjos
A	Seven Bagatelles	Kjos

Berger, Jean (born 1909) U.S.A.

E	Country Sketches	Kjos
I	Diversions for Keyboard	Kjos
I	More Diversions for Keyboard	Kjos
I	Sonatina	Presser

Berkowitz, Sol (U.S.A.)

E-I	Jazzettes	Galaxy
E-I	Nine Folk Song Preludes	Frank

Berlin, Boris (born 1907) Canada (born Russia)

E-I	Piano Highlights, Vols. 1, 2	Frederick Harris

Bernstein, Leonard (1918-1991) U.S.A.

I-A		Five Anniversaries	Schirmer
I-A		Four Anniversaries	Schirmer

Bernstein, Seymour (born 1927) U.S.A.

E		Birds, Vols. I, II	Schroder & Gunther
I		Belinda the Chipmunk	Schirmer
I		Moodscapes	Schirmer

Binkerd, Gordon (born 1916) U.S.A.

E		Piano Miscellany	Boosey & Hawkes
E	§	The Young Pianist	Boosey & Hawkes
E-I		Entertainments for Piano	Boosey & Hawkes
A	*	Concert Set (Etude, Mice)	Boosey & Hawkes

Britten, (Edward) Benjamin (1913-1976) England

I		Walztes [sic] Op. 3	Faber
A		Three Character Pieces (1930)	Faber

Campbell, Carolyn Jones (U.S.A.)

I		7 Preludes for Keyboard	Willis

Caramia, Tony (born 1950) U.S.A.

E	§	Folksongs Revisited	New School
E	§	Sounds of Jazz, Vols. I, II	New School
E-I		Rag Times Four (3 solos, 1 duet)	Kjos
I		Adventures in Jazz Piano, Vols. I, II	Bärenreiter
I		Classic Pops	Hal Leonard
I		Jazz Moods for the Pianist	Belwin
I		Jazz Right Now!	Belwin
I		Jazz Sampler	Belwin
I		OK Jazz!	Belwin
I		Pieces of Blue	Belwin
I		Romantic Pops	Hal Leonard
I		Six Sketches	New School
I		Toccata	Myklas
I-A	§	Excursions in Jazz Styles	Kendor
I-A		Fascinatin' Rhythms	Kjos

Casadesus, Robert (1899-1972) France

I		6 Enfantines Op. 48	Durand
I-A		24 Préludes, Vols. I-IV	Max Eschig

Casella, Alfredo (1883-1947) Italy

I		11 Pièces Enfantines Op. 35 (1920)	Universal

Chagy, John (U.S.A.)

I	Atlanta Sonatina	Myklas
I	Ballet Sonatina	Myklas
I	Etude Baroque	Fischer
I	Ragtime Festival	Myklas
I	Razz-Ma-Jazz	Kjos
A	Peachtree Street Rag	Kjos

Chatman, Stephen (born 1950) Canada (born U.S.A.)

E-I	Amusements, Books 2, 3	Frederick Harris

Chávez, Carlos (1899-1978) Mexico

I-A	Sonatina	Arrow
I-A	Ten Preludes	Schirmer

Clarke, Lucia (U.S.A.)

I	Jazz and all that!, Vols. I, II	Myklas

Colley, Betty (U.S.A.)

E		Reflections at the Piano	Kjos
E	§	Styles for Piano	Kjos
I		Takin' It Easy	Kjos

Copland, Aaron (1900-1991) U.S.A.

E			In Evening Air	Boosey & Hawkes
E			Midsummer Nocturne	Boosey & Hawkes
E			Three Moods	Boosey & Hawkes
E			Two Children's Pieces (Sunday Afternoon Music, The Young Pioneers)	Fischer
I			Scherzo Humoristique (The Cat and the Mouse) (1920)	Durand
I-A	§	*	Four Piano Blues (1, 3)	Boosey & Hawkes
I-A			Two Piano Pieces	Boosey & Hawkes
A			Passacaglia	Salabert
A			Piano Album	Boosey & Hawkes

Corea, Chick (born 1941) U.S.A.

I	Children's Songs (20 Pieces)	Schott

Cowell, Henry (1897-1965) U.S.A.

I	Bounce Dance	Merion
I	Sway Dance	Presser
I	The Irishman Dances	Fischer
I	The Irish Minstrel Sings	Fischer
I-A	Piano Works	Associated

Creston, Paul (1906-1985) U.S.A.

I		Five Dances Op. 1 (1946)	Shawnee
I		Five Little Dances Op. 24	Schirmer
I-A		Rhythmicon	Colombo
A		Six Preludes Op. 39	Schirmer

Dallapiccola, Luigi (1904-1975) Italy

A	Quaderno Musicale de Annalibera (1953)	Suvini Zerboni

Danna, Mychael (born 1958) Canada

E	Land of Narnia	Frederick Harris

Dello Joio, Norman (born 1913) U.S.A.

E	§		Suite for the Young (10 easy pieces)	Schirmer
E-I	§	*	Lyric Pieces for the Young (Prayer of the Matador, Street Cries)	Marks
I			Diversions	Marks
I			Prelude: To a Young Dancer	Schirmer
I	§		Prelude: To a Young Musician	Schirmer
A			Suite for the Piano	Schirmer

Diamond, David (born 1915) U.S.A.

E	Eight Piano Pieces	Schirmer
E-I	Alone at the Piano (3 books)	Peer Southern
I	Album for the Young	Elkan-Vogel

Diemer, Emma Lou (born 1927) U.S.A.

E-I	Adventures in Sound	Summy-Birchard
E-I	Sound Pictures	Boosey & Hawkes
I-A	Three Pieces for Piano	Plymouth
I-A	Toccata for Piano	Sisra

Dittenhaver, Sarah Louise (U.S.A.)

E	Appalachian Mountain Melody	Kjos
E	Circus Day	Kjos
E	Sea Winds	Kjos
E	Spring Breezes	Kjos
E	The Marching Band	Kjos
I	Appalachian Reverie	Kjos
I	Coney Island Spring	Kjos

Dring, Madeleine (1923-1977) Great Britain

I	A Colour Suite	Arcadia
I	Three Dances: Mazurka, Pavane, and Landler	Cambria

Dubois, Pierre Max (born 1930) France

I	Esquisses (1961)	Alphonse Leduc

Dutkiewicz, Andrzej (born 1942) U.S.A. (born Poland)

E	The Puppet Suite	Kjos
E	Seascapes	Kjos
A	Toccatina and Suite for Piano	Kjos

Eckhardt-Gramatté, Sophie-Carmen (1899-1974) Canada (born Russia)

I-A	"From My Childhood": Alphabet Pieces, Vol. I	Waterloo
I-A	"From My Childhood": Character Pieces, Vol. II	Waterloo

Evans, Bill (1929-1980) U.S.A.

A	The Artistry of Bill Evans (Blancq ed.)	Belwin
A	Solo Transcriptions (5 volumes)	TRO Ludlow

Evans, Bill G. (U.S.A.)

I	Jazzettes	Kjos
I	Jazz Sweets	Kjos

Evans, Lee (U.S.A.)

E	§	More! Jack and Jill Jazz	Hal Leonard
E	§	Tickle the Ivories	Hal Leonard
I		The Elements of Jazz	Hal Leonard
I	§	Jazzmatazz	Hal Leonard
I		Jazz Suite	Hal Leonard
I		Rock Styles for Piano	Hal Leonard
I		Travel the Keyboard Jazz Highway	Hal Leonard
I		Watercolors	Hal Leonard
I-A		Advanced Rock Styles for Piano	Hal Leonard
I-A	§	Easy Jazz Standards	Hal Leonard
I-A		Jazz Giants	Hal Leonard
I-A		Jazz Greats	Hal Leonard
I-A	§	Lee Evans Arranges:	Hal Leonard
		Cole Porter	
		George Gershwin	
		Jerome Kern	
I-A	§	More Easy Jazz Standards	Hal Leonard
I-A		Stephen Sondheim	Hal Leonard
A		Carnival Suite	Hal Leonard
A		Celebration Suite	Hal Leonard
A		Famous Jazz Piano Styles	Hal Leonard
A		Introduction & Toccata in Jazz	Hal Leonard

Faith, Richard (born 1926) U.S.A.

I	Finger Paintings (1968)	Shawnee
I	Three Sonatinas (1971)	Schirmer

Feliciano, Richard (U.S.A.)

E-I	Two Hearts	Schirmer

Fennimore, Joseph (U.S.A.)

I	Canon and Cannon	Marks

Fernandez, Oscar Lorenzo (1897-1948) Brazil

I		Children's Visions (3 pieces)	Peer International
I		Dolls (5 pieces)	Peer International
I	§	Suite das 5 Notas (8 short pieces)	Peer International
I		Yaya, The Doll	Peer International

Finney, Ross Lee (born 1906) U.S.A.

E	§	Games (32 short pieces)	Peters
I		Inventions (24 pieces)	Peters
I		Youth's Companion	Peters
A	*	Nostalgic Waltzes (5 Waltzes, No. 1)	Mercury

Fischer, Edwin (1886-1960) Switzerland

I	Sonatina in C	Ries & Erler

Floyd, Carlisle (born 1926) U.S.A.

E-I	Episodes, Vols. I, II	Boosey & Hawkes

Françaix, Jean (born 1912) France

I-A §	The Françaix Collection (Hinson ed.)	Schott

Francois, Claudine (France)

I	Piano Jazz	Lemoine

Freed, Isadore (1900-1960) U.S.A. (born Russia)

E	Inca War Song	Presser
E	Waltz on the White Keys	Presser
I	Pastorales (8 small pieces)	E C Schirmer

Frerichs, Doris (U.S.A.)

I	A Royal Suite	Willis

Fuleihan, Anis (1900-1970) U.S.A. (born Greece)

I	Around the Clock (12 preludes)	Southern
I	Fifteen Short Pieces	Fischer
I	Five Very Short Pieces for Talented Young Bipeds	Peer International

Ganz, Rudolph (1877-1972) U.S.A. (born Switzerland)

E-I	Animal Pictures	Fischer

George, Jon (U.S.A.)

E	A Day in the Forest	Summy-Birchard
E	A Day in the Jungle	Summy-Birchard
E	Six Sonatinas	Alfred
E-I §	Kaleidoscope Solos, Vols. III, IV, V	Alfred

Gershwin, George (1898-1937) U.S.A.

I	George Gershwin for Piano	Hal Leonard
I-A	Music by Gershwin	Warner
A	A Tribute to George Gershwin (Coates ed.)	Warner
A	Blue Monday (arr. Zizzo)	Warner
A	George Gershwin for Piano	Chappell
A	Gershwin at the Keyboard (18 song arrangements)	Warner
A	Impromptu in Two Keys	New World
A	Jazz Interpretations	Warner
A § *	Preludes (2, 1, 3)	New World
A § *	Song Arrangements (Do It Again, Somebody Loves Me, Swanee)	New World
A	Two Waltzes in C	Warner

Gillock, William (born 1917) U.S.A.

E §	Accent on Solos, Vol. III	Willis
E-I §	Accent on Analytical Sonatinas	Willis
I	Fanfare & Other Courtly Scenes in Baroque Style	Summy-Birchard
I	Flamenco	Willis
I §	Lyric Preludes in Romantic Style	Summy-Birchard
I §	New Orleans Jazz Styles	Willis
I	More New Orleans Jazz Styles	Willis
I	Still More New Orleans Jazz Styles	Willis
I	Nocturne	Schirmer
I	Polynesian Nocturne	Willis
I	Sonatine	Willis
I §	Sonatina in Classic Style	Willis
I §	Three Jazz Preludes	Willis

Ginastera, Alberto (Evaristo) (1916-1983) Argentina

I	Rondo on Argentine Children's Folk Tunes	Boosey & Hawkes
I-A §	Twelve American Preludes, Vols. I, II	Fischer
A	Danzas Argentinas (3 dances)	Durand

Glover, David Carr (1925-1988) U.S.A.

I §	The Great Smoky Mountains	Belwin

Goldston, Margaret (U.S.A.)

E		Windows	Galaxy
I		Carnival Capers	Alfred
I		Seasons	Alfred

Grainger, (George) Percy (Aldridge) (1882-1961) U.S.A. (born Australia)

I	§	Country Gardens	Schirmer
A		Percy Grainger Piano Album	Schirmer

Granados, (y Campiña) Enrique (1867-1916) Spain

A		Twelve Spanish Dances (4 books)	International

Gretchaninoff, Alexander Tikhonovich (1864-1956) Russia
    (Grechaninov)

E		Children's Book Op. 98 (Palmer ed.)	Alfred
E		Five Miniatures for Piano Op. 196	Marks
E		Glass Beads Op. 123 (12 easy pieces) (Palmer ed.)	Alfred
E		Grandfather's Book Op. 119 (17 easy pieces)	Schott
I		Eight Pastels Op. 61	Kalmus
I		The Gretchaninoff Collection (Hinson ed.)	Schott

Grill, Joyce (U.S.A.)

I	§	Thanks, Anna Magdalena	Belwin

Grove, Roger (U.S.A.)

E		Jazz About	Kjos
E	§	Riches of Rags	Summy-Birchard
I		Celebration	Pro Art
I		Light Blue	Summy-Birchard

Hanson, Howard (1896-1981) U.S.A.

I	The Bell	Fischer
I	Dance of the Warriors	Fischer
I	The Eccentric Clock	Fischer
I	Enchantment	Fischer
A	Three Miniatures	Fischer

Harris, Roy (1898-1979) U.S.A.

A	American Ballads	Fischer
A	Little Suite for Piano	Schirmer

Hartsell, Randall

E	New Beginnings	Alfred
E	Something Special	Alfred
E-I	Moments to Remember, Books 1, 2	Alfred

Hawes, Jack (born 1916) England

I	Nocturne	Fischer

Heiss, John (born 1938) U.S.A.

I	Four Short Pieces	Boosey & Hawkes

Hergo, Jane

I	Keyboard Confections (6 pieces)	Belwin

Hindemith, Paul (1895-1963) Germany

E	Wir bauen eine Stadt (Let's Build a City)	Schott
I	The Hindemith Collection (Hinson ed.)	Schott
I	Kleine Klaviermusik	Schott
A	Ludus Tonalis (Studies in Counterpoint, Tonal Organization and Piano Playing) (1943)	Schott
A	Sonata No. 2	Schott

Honegger, Arthur (1892-1955) Switzerland (born France)

I	Souvenir de Chopin	Choudens
I-A	Piano Album	Salabert

Hovhaness, Alan (born 1911) U.S.A. (Armenian heritage)
(Chakmakjian, Alan Hovhaness)

E	Sketchbook of Mr. Purple Poverty	Broude
I	Mountain Idylls (Moon Lullaby, Moon Dance, Mountain Lullaby)	Associated
I	Mystic Flute Op. 22	Peters
I	Slumber Song, Siris' Dance Op. 52, Nos. 2, 3	MCA
I	Twelve Armenian Folk Songs Op. 43	Peters
I	Two Ghazals Op. 36	Peters

Janácek, Leos (1854-1928) Czechoslovakia

I-A	By the Overgrown Tracks (53 pieces in 2 books) (1902 and 1908)	Artia

Joplin, Scott (1868-1917) U.S.A.
(Known in the late 19th Century as "King of Ragtime")

A	An Adventure in Ragtime	Belwin
A	At the Piano with Joplin (Hinson ed.)	Alfred
A	Collected Piano Works	Belwin
A	Complete Piano Rags	Dover
A	Selected Favorite Rags (Hinson ed.)	Alfred

Kabalevsky, Dmitri Borisovich (1904-1987) Russia

E	28 Piano Pieces (Kabalevskaya [Kabalevsky's daughter] ed.)	Hal Leonard
E-I	Fifteen Children's Pieces Op. 27, Book 1	MCA
E-I	Ten Children's Pieces Op. 27, Book 2	MCA

E-I §	Kabalevsky: Young Pianist's Guide to the Great Composers (Novik ed.)	Belwin
E-I §	30 Piano Pieces Op. 27 (Palmer ed.)	Alfred
E-I	Twenty-Four Little Pieces Op. 39	Schirmer
I	At the Piano with Kabalevsky (Hinson ed.)	Alfred
I	Five Easy Sets of Variations Op. 51	MCA
I	Four Little Pieces Op. 14	MCA
I	Four Preludes Op. 5	MCA
I	Sonatinas Op. 13 No. 1, 2	MCA
I	Sonatinas for Piano Op. 13 (Palmer ed.)	Alfred
I §	Toccatina	MCA
I	Variations Op. 40 (2 sets)	MCA
I-A	Twenty-Four Preludes Op. 38	MCA
A	Four Rondos Op. 60	MCA

Karp, David (U.S.A.)

E	A Day at the Zoo	Willis
E	Adventure in Sound	Willis
E	Escapades	Shawnee
E-I	Jubilant Sounds	Alfred
I §	Shades of Time	Alfred

Kennan, Kent (born 1913) U.S.A.

I-A	Retrospectives	Schirmer
A §	Three Preludes for the Piano (1941)	Schirmer

Khachaturian, Aram Il'yich (1903-1978) Russia

E	Album for Young People, Vol. I (Palmer ed.)	Alfred
I §	Adventures of Ivan	MCA
I	Children's Album, Vols. I, II	Peters
I §	Sonatina (1959)	Alfred
A	Toccata	MCA

Kocour, Mike (U.S.A.)

I §	Cool Jazz, Books 1, 2	Belwin

Kodály, Zoltán (1881-1967) Hungary

E	Twenty-four Little Canons on the Black Keys	Boosey & Hawkes
I	Gyermektáncok [Children's Dances]	Boosey & Hawkes

Konowitz, Bert (U.S.A.)

I	Jazz for Piano (Pace ed.)	Lee Roberts

Kowalchyk, Gayle / E. L. Lancaster,(U. S. A.)

E §	Boogie 'n' Blues	Alfred

Kraehenbuehl, David (U.S.A.)

E		Elegy	Summy-Birchard
E	§	Patterns In Blue	Keyboard Arts
E		Spanish Waltz	Summy-Birchard

Krenek, Ernst (born 1900) U.S.A. (born Austria)

A	Twelve Short Piano Pieces Op. 83	Schirmer

Kubik, Gail Thompson (1914-1984) U.S.A.

I	Dance Soliloquy	Mercury
I	Quiet Time	Presser
A	Sonatina	Mercury

La Montaine, John (born 1920) U.S.A.

I	A Child's Picture Book	Broude Brothers
A	Toccata Op. 1	Broude Brothers

Labúnski, Wiktor (born 1895) U.S.A. (born Poland)

I	§	Four Variations on a Theme by Paganini	Fischer

Last, Joan (England)

E	On the Move (7 solos)	Boosey & Hawkes
I	Petites Images (5 solos)	Boosey & Hawkes

Lauer, Elizabeth (U.S.A.)

E	Soundings	Fischer

Lecuona, Ernesto (1896-1963) Cuba

I	Malagueña	Marks
I	Suite Espagnole (6 pieces)	Marks

Lees, Benjamin (born 1925) U.S.A. (born China)

A	Fantasia	Boosey & Hawkes

Leighton, Kenneth (born 1929) Great Britain

I	8 Pieces for Angela Op. 47	Novello

Lutoslawski, Witold (born 1913) Poland

I	Popular Melodies of Poland (12 easy pieces)	Polskie Wydawnictwo

Martin, Frank (1890-1974) Switzerland

A	Eight Preludes for Piano	Universal

Martin, Jean (U.S.A.)

E		Festive Fantasies	Kjos
E		Foreign Flavors	Kjos
E		Holiday Dreams	Kjos
E		Kaleidoscope	Kjos
E	§	Parisian Images	Kjos
E		Post Cards from Abroad	Kjos
E-I		Country Charms	Kjos
I		Enchanted Forest	Kjos
I	§	New York City Scenes	Kjos

Mathers, Carolyn (U.S.A.)

I	Ash Tree Collection	Myklas

Mauldin, Michael (U.S.A.)

E	Five Preludes for Synthesizer	Kjos
E	Impressions for Synthesizer and Piano	Kjos
I	Outside Images	Kjos

Meeker, Eugenie (U.S.A.)

E	Piano Scenes for the Young	Kjos

Mehegan, John (U.S.A.)

I-A	Tonal and Rhythmic Principles, Book 1	Watson-Guptill
I-A	Jazz Rhythm and the Improvised Line, Book 2	Watson-Guptill
I-A	Swing and Early Progressive Piano Styles, Book 3	Watson-Guptill
I-A	Contemporary Piano Styles (Jazz improvisation), Book 4	Watson-Guptill

Menotti, Gian Carlo (born 1911) U.S.A. (born Italy)

I	§	Poemetti (1937) (12 pieces)	Ricordi

Messiaen, Olivier (Eugène Prosper Charles) (1908-1992) France

A	*	Préludes (No. 7)	Durand

Middlebrook, Mamie (U.S.A.)

I	Indian Summer	Boston

Mier, Martha (U.S.A.)

E	Holiday Treats	Alfred
I	Celebrate America!	Alfred

Milhaud, Darius (1892-1974) France

I	Accueil Amical: Pièces enfantines	Heugel
I-A	Saudades do Brasil Op. 67 (Suite of Dances, Books I, II)	Max Eschig

Miller, Beatrice (U.S.A.)

I	French Carousel	New School
I	Morning and Evening	New School
I-A	Little Rhapsody	New School

Mompou, Federico (1893-1987) Spain

I	Charmes	Max Eschig
I	Quatre Préludes	Heugel
I	Scènes d'Enfants (1915)	Salabert

Muczynski, Robert (born 1929) U.S.A.

E		Fables		Schirmer
I		Diversions Op. 23		Schirmer
I-A		A Summer Journal Op. 19		Schirmer
I-A		Collected Piano Pieces		Schirmer
A	§	*	Six Preludes Op. 6 (1, 6)	Schirmer
A		Suite Op. 13		Schirmer

Murow, Christine (U.S.A.)

E	Voices of Invention	Myklas

Niamath, Linda (born 1939) Canada

E	Marching Mice and Other Pieces	Frederick Harris
E	Soda Pop and Other Delights	Frederick Harris
E	A Zoo For You	Frederick Harris
E-I	Fancy Free	Frederick Harris

Nibley, Reid (U.S.A.)

I	Reflection	Kjos

Norton, Christopher (born 1953) U.S.A.

I	Microstyles for Keyboard, Books 1, 2	Boosey & Hawkes

O'Hearn, Arletta (U.S.A.)

E		Blues and Other Colors	Kjos
E	§	Love Jazz	Kjos
E		Sunshine and Blues	Kjos
I		In a Jazz Groove	Kjos
I		Swing Street	Kjos
A	§	Three Piano Preludes in Jazz Stylings	Kjos

Olson, Kevin R. (born 1970) U.S.A.

I	Clown Chase	Frederick Harris
I-A	Toccata in D	Frederick Harris

Olson, Lynn Freeman (1938-1987) U.S.A.

E		Beginning Sonatinas	Alfred
E		Lazy Bayou Blues	Alfred
E	§	Menagerie	Oxford
E		Willows In the Rain	Alfred
E-I		Audience Pleasers I, II, III	Alfred
E-I		Four Sonatinas in Varying Styles	Alfred
I	§	Adventures in Style	Fischer
I	§	Finger Progress	Fischer
I	§	Piano Favorites, Book 2	Fischer

Paderewski, Ignace Jan (1860-1941) Poland

I	§	Menuet Op. 14 No. 1	Schirmer

Palmer, Willard Aldrich, Jr. (born 1917) U.S.A.

E	§	Baroque Folk	Alfred
E		Nine Blind Mice	Alfred

Pearce, Elvina Truman (U.S.A)

E		Excursions	Belwin
E		Seven Preludes	Belwin
E	§	Solo Flight	New School
E	§	Sound Reflections, Vols. I, II	Alfred
E-I		4 O'clock Tunes	New School
I		Effective Sounds (7 Pieces for Piano)	Bradley
I		Expressions	Belwin
I		Seven Preludes in Seven Keys, Book 2	Belwin

Peeters, Flor (1903-1986) Belgium

I		Ten Bagatelles Op. 88	Peters

Persichetti, Vincent (1915-1987) U.S.A.

E		Little Mirror Book	Elkan-Vogel
E		Little Piano Book Op. 60 (14 short pieces)	Elkan-Vogel
E	§	Parades Op. 57 (March, Canter, Pomp)	Elkan-Vogel
E		Serenade No. 7 Op. 55	Elkan-Vogel
I		Six Sonatinas, Vols. I, II	Elkan-Vogel
I-A		Poems Op. 4; Op. 5, Vols. I, II	Elkan-Vogel

Pinto, Octavio (1890-1950) Brazil

E		Festa de Crianças (Children's Festival)	Schirmer
I		Marcha do Pequeña Polegar (Tom Thumb's March)	Schirmer
I	§	Scenas Infantis (5 descriptive scenes)	Schirmer

Piston, Walter (1894-1976) U.S.A.

I		Improvisation	MCA

Poe, John Robert (U.S.A.)

E		Circuit Breakers	Kjos
E		Look to the Skies	Myklas
E		Mostly Monsters	Myklas
E		Poepourri	Myklas
E		Safari	Fischer
E	§	Sea Pictures	Fischer
I		American Folk Songs	Myklas

Poulenc, Francis (Jean Marcel) (1899-1963) France

I		Feuillets d'Album (Ariette, Rêve, Gigue) (1933)	Salabert
I		Pastourelle	Heugel
I		Villageoises (5 pieces for young people)	Salabert
I-A		Suite (1920)	Durand
I-A	§	Mouvements Perpétuels (3 pieces) (1918)	Chester
A		Album of Six Pieces	Chester
A		Suite Française d'après Claude Gervaise (1935)	Durand
A		Trois Novelettes	Chester
A	§	Trois Pièces (Pastorale, Toccata, Hymne)	Heugel

Previn, André (born 1929) U.S.A. (born Germany)

I		Birthday Party	Robbins
I	§	Impressions for Piano	MCA

Prokofiev, Sergey (Sergeyevich) (1891-1953) Russia

E-I	§	*	Music for Children Op. 65	Boosey & Hawkes
			(The Rain and the Rainbow, Tarantella, Waltz)	
I			Sonatine Pastorale (from Op. 59)	Boosey & Hawkes
I			Tales of the Old Grandmother Op. 31	Leeds
I-A			Sarcasms Op. 17	Boosey & Hawkes
I-A			Selected Works (Baylor ed.)	Alfred
I-A			Shorter Piano Works	Dover
I-A	§	*	Visions fugitives Op. 22 (1, 2, 16) (Baylor ed.)	Alfred; Boosey & Hawkes
A			Four Pieces Op. 4	Leeds
A		*	Nine Sonatas (1, 3)	Boosey & Hawkes

Ptaszynska, Marta (born 1943) Poland

E-I	Miniatures	Belwin

Richie, Marjorie (U.S.A).

I	Jazz Solos	Alfred

Rochberg, George (born 1918) U.S.A.

A	§	Twelve Bagatelles	Presser

Rocherolle, Eugenie R. (U.S.A.)

E			Classical Theme & Variations	Kjos
E			Westwinds	Kjos
I	§		American Sampler	Kjos
I			Bayou Reflections	Kjos
I			Blockbuster!	Kjos
I			Discoveries	Kjos
I			Extravaganza	Kjos
I			Getting Into Intervals	Kjos
I			Hands Separately	Kjos
I			Just for Friends	Kjos
I			Keepsakes	Kjos
I			Miniatures	Kjos
I	§		Montage	Kjos
I			New Orleans Remembered	Kjos
I			Pages from a Scrapbook	Kjos
I			Seven Scenes	Kjos
l			Simple Pleasures	Kjos
I	§	*	Six Moods for Piano (Downstream)	Kjos
I			Sonatina in C	Kjos
I			Souvenirs du Chateau	Kjos
I			Vintage Favorites	Kjos

Rodrigo, Joaquín (born 1901) Spain

I-A	The Rodrigo Collection (10 piano works) (Hinson ed.)	Schott

Rollin, Catherine (U.S.A.)

I	§	Preludes for Piano, Vols. I, II	Alfred
I		Spotlight on Baroque Style	Alfred
I		Spotlight on Classical Style	Alfred
I		Spotlight on Jazz Style	Alfred
I		Spotlight on Ragtime Style	Alfred
I		Spotlight on Romantic Style	Alfred
I-A		The New Virtuoso	Alfred

Rorem, Ned (born 1923) U.S.A.

I	A Quiet Afternoon	Peer International
I-A	Three Barcarolles	Peters

Rubenstein, Beryl (1898-1952) U.S.A.

E	§	A Day in the Country (5 impromptus)	Fischer
I		Twelve Definitions	Schirmer

Sanucci, Frank (U.S.A.)

I	§	American Scene	Willis
I		Western Holiday	Willis

Schoenberg, Arnold (Franz Walter) (1874-1951) Germany

I	*	Sechs kleine Klavierstücke Op. 19 Nos. 2, 6	Universal

Schonthal, Ruth (U.S.A.)

E	Bird Calls	Oxford

Schuman, William Howard (1910-1992) U.S.A.

I	Three Moods	Presser
I	Three Score Set (1943)	Schirmer

Schwenk, Deborah (U.S.A.)

I	Penguin Parade	New School

Scriabin, Alexander (1872-1915) Russia

A		Preludes and Poems	Peters
A		Selected Works (Baylor ed.)	Alfred
A	*	The Complete Preludes and Etudes (Op. 2 Nos. 2, 15)	Dover
A		Twenty-Four Preludes Op. 11	Peters

Sculthorpe, Peter Joshua (born 1929) Australia

I	Night Pieces	Faber

Sessions, Roger (1896-1985) U.S.A.

I	March	Fischer
I	Scherzino	Fischer

Shaak, Bernard (U.S.A.)

E-I	§	Events, Vols. III, IV	Moonstone

Sheftel, Paul (U.S.A.)

E		Easy as ABC	Alfred
E		Easy as 1, 2, 3	Alfred
E		Keyboard Karnival	Alfred
E	§	Patterns for Fun, Books 1, 2	Alfred
E		Sightreading Folk Songs from Around the World, I, II, III	Alfred
E-I		"I Haven't Practiced..."	Alfred
E-I		Modules	Alfred
I		Blues and All That Jazz	Alfred
I		Blues for Fun	Alfred
I	§	Etudes Brutus	Alfred
I		Folk Songs from Around the World, Vols. I-III	Alfred
I	§	Interludes	Fischer
I		Merry and Mellow	Alfred
I		One plus One	Alfred
I		Paul's Practical Piano Pieces	Alfred

I		Play's the Thing	Alfred
I	§	Preludes, Interludes, and a Postlude	Alfred
I-A		Paul's Perplexing Piano Pieces	Alfred

Shostakovich, Dmitry (1906-1975) Russia
(Dmitriyevich)

E	§	Six Children's Pieces	MCA
E		Puppets' Dances	Peters
I		Doll's Dances (7 easy pieces)	MCA
I-A		Five Preludes	MCA
I-A		Twenty-Four Preludes Op. 34	Peters
A		Three Fantastic Dances Op. 5 (Hinson ed.)	Alfred

Siegmeister, Elie (born 1909) U.S.A.

E		The Children's Day	MCA
I	§	Americana Kaleidoscope	Sam Fox

Sowerby, Leo (1895-1968) U.S.A.

I		A Fancy	Presser

Starer, Robert (born 1924) U.S.A. (born Austria)

E		Seven Vignettes	Leeds
I	§	Sketches in Color, Vols. I, II	MCA
E-A		Album for Piano (complete piano works)	Hal Leonard
A		Excursions for a Pianist	MCA

Stevens, Halsey (1908-1988) U.S.A.

E	Five Little Five Finger Exercises	Helios
E	Six Russian Folktunes	ACA
E	Ten French Folksongs	ACA
E	Ten Short Pieces	ACA
I	Five Swedish Folk Tunes	Helios
I	Jumping Colts	Helios
I-A	17 Piano Pieces	Westwood
A	5 Portuguese Folksongs	Peer International

Stewart, Frank (U.S.A.)

A	Toccata	Kjos

Stravinsky, Igor (Fyodorovich) (1882-1971)
(Russian composer, later of French (1934) and American (1945) nationality)

E	Les Cinq Doigts	Mercury

Stravinsky, Soulima (born 1910) U.S.A. (born Switzerland)

E-I	Piano Music for Children, Vols. I, II	Peters
I	6 Easy Sonatinas for Young Pianists	Peters

Sumera, Lepo (born 1950) Estonia

I   Three Piano Pieces for Children   Schirmer

Strommen, Carl (U.S.A.)

E §   Piano a la . . . Jazz, Easy   Alfred
I §   Piano a la . . . Jazz, Intermediate   Alfred

Tajčevič, Marko (1900-1984) Yugoslavia

E §   Kleine S tücke für Klavier   Henle

Takács, Jenö (born 1902) Hungary

I   Something New for You   Doblinger

Tansman, Alexandre (1897-1986) France (born Poland)

E-I   Pour les Enfants   Max Eschig
I   Ten Diversions for the Young Pianist   Associated

Tcherepnin, Alexander (Nikolayevich) (1899-1977) U.S.A. (born Russia)

I   Bagatelles Chinoises Op. 51 No. 3   Heugel
I   Episodes (12 sketches)   Heugel
I   Expressions Op. 81   Leeds
I   Pour Petits et Grands, Vols. I, II   Durand
I-A §   Bagatelles Op. 5 (Olson ed.)   Alfred

Telfer, Nancy (born 1950) Canada

E   I'm Not Scared   Frederick Harris
E   Put on your Dancing Shoes   New School
E-I   Old Tales in a New Guise   Frederick Harris

Thompson, John (U.S.A.)

E   From Foreign Shores   Frederick Harris

Thompson, Randall (1899-1984) U.S.A.

I §   Little Prelude   Fischer
I   Seven Musical Travelogues [out of print]   Frederick Harris

Toch, Ernst (1887-1964) Austria (naturalized American)

E-A   Five Times Ten Studies for Piano (or Fünfmal zehn Etüden für Klavier)   Schott
I-A   Burlesken Op. 31 No. 3 (The Juggler)   Schott

Tsitsaros, Christos (born 1961) Cyprus

E-I §	The Bike Ride	Hal Leonard
I-A	Autumn Sketches (6 Pieces)	Hal Leonard
A	Blackbirds at Ueno (Concert Etude)	Hal Leonard

Turina, Joaquín (1882-1949) Spain

I	Miniatures	Schott
I-A	Album de Viaje (5 Travel Impressions)	Belwin
I-A	Danzas Gitanas Op. 55, Vols. I, II (5 pieces each volume)	Salabert
I-A	The Turina Collection, 20 Pieces (Hinson ed.)	Schott
A §	The Circus (Clowns) (1932)	Schott

Vandall, Robert D. (U.S.A.)

E		Short Suite	Myklas
E		Vandall Stylings U. S. A.	Myklas
E-I	§	Bagatelles, Vols. I, II	Myklas
E-I		Modes and Moods	Myklas
I	§	American Folk Songs	Myklas
I		Cloudy Day	Myklas
I		Diversion	Boston
I		Hommage to Scarlatti	Myklas
I		Jazz Sonatina	Bradley
I	§	Movin'	Myklas
I	§	Preludes, Vols. I, II	Myklas
I		Remembrance	Myklas
I		Reverie	Myklas
I		White Heat	Myklas
A		Circles	Boston
A	§	Preludes, Vol. III	Myklas

Victor, Janine (France)

E	§	Delphine au Piano (3 pieces)	Zurfluh

Villa-Lobos, Heitor (1887-1959) Brazil

I		Petizado	Peer International
I		Ten Pieces on Popular Children's Folk Tunes	Mercury
I		The Three Maries - Amitak, Alnilam, Mintika	Fischer
I-A	§	Prole do Bébé (The Baby's Dolls) (8 pieces including "O Polichinello")	Marks

Ward-Steinman, David (born 1936) U.S.A.

I	Improvisations on Children's Songs	Lee Roberts
I	Three Miniatures	Facsimile Edition

Watson-Henderson, Ruth (born 1932) Canada

I	Six Miniatures for Piano	Frederick Harris

Waxman, Donald (U.S.A.)

E-I §	Pageants for Piano	Galaxy

Willan, Healey (1880-1968) Canada

E-I	Graded Studies for Piano	Frederick Harris

Wuensch, Gerhard (born 1925) Canada (born Austria)

E-I §	Ping Pong Anyone? (9 solos)	Frederick Harris

Yarmolinsky, Ben

E	Four Pieces for Piano (Pastorale, Nocturne, Dance, and Finale)	Schirmer

Yeager, Jeanine (U.S.A.)

E		Especially for You	Kjos
E		Just for Fun	Kjos
E		Roundup Ranch	Kjos
E		Solitudes	Kjos
E		Technique Teasers	Kjos
I		Around the Sundial	Kjos
I		Classic Inspirations	Kjos
I		Déjà Vu	Kjos
I		Mostly Mellow	Kjos
I	§	Quiet Moods	Kjos
I		Smart Moves	Kjos
I		Strike It Rich, Vols. I, II	Kjos
I		Too Hot to Handle	Kjos
I-A		Sincerely Yours	Kjos

Twentieth Century or Jazz Collections and Anthologies

A Contemporary Album for the Young (Palmer ed.) Alfred

The Best of Ragtime (Morath ed.) TRO

The Best of Scott Joplin (Ryerson ed.) Hansen

§ Blue Ribbon Series: Favorite Piano Solos, Vols. I-IV (Flatau ed.) Belwin
Elementary and early intermediate solos by 20th-century educational composers who
specialize in writing compositions for young piano students.

§ Bravo Brazil!, Vols. I, II (Appleby ed.) Kjos
(16 and 24 pages) A unique collection of early intermediate to late intermediate
compositions by Brazilian composers. Includes composers such as Ernst Mahle, Marlos
Nobre, Heitor Villa-Lobos, and Camargo Guarnieri.

Classic Piano Rags (Blesh ed.) Dover

Contempo Series (M. Clark ed.) Myklas
    Contempo 1
    Contempo 2
    Contempos in Jade
    Contempos in Crimson
    Contempos in Sapphire
    Contempos in Orchid
    In the Mode

Contemporary Music and the Pianist (Canaday ed.) Alfred

§ Contemporary Piano Literature, Vols. I-VI (F. Clark ed.) Summy-Birchard
(Volumes range from 24 to 64 pages.) One of the first published collections
of carefully graded contemporary 20th-century teaching pieces.

Contemporary Russian Composers Schirmer

§ Cream of the Crop, Vols. I, II Summy-Birchard
(32 pages each) Includes popular teaching pieces by 20th-century educational
composers such as Katherine Beard, Roger Grove, David Karp, and William Gillock.

Favorite Piano Solos, Vols. I-III (Flatau ed.) Belwin

51 Piano Pieces Schirmer

Five-Finger Music Summy-Birchard

§ From Russia For Youth (Boris Berlin ed.) Frederick Harris
(24 pages) 28 early intermediate contemporary pieces by Russian composers
including Kabalevsky, Salutrinskaya, Tchaikovsky, Khachaturian, Lubarsky,
Barenboim and Lukomsky.

§ Harris Piano Classics - Romantic & 20th Century Repertoire Frederick Harris
(Volumes 1b-7b range from 16 to 24 pages and include 9-12 piano compositions
each.) Graded piano pieces include composers from all style periods. "b" volumes
contain Romantic and 20th-century repertoire.

Jazz and Blues, Books 5, 6 (Kraehenbuehl arr.) Summy-Birchard

Jazz Piano Solos for any Beginner Bradley

Jazz Piano Transcribed Solos (Priestley ed.) Hal Leonard

The Joy of Boogie and Blues (Agay/Martin arr.)	Yorktown
The Joy of Ragtime (Agay ed.)	Yorktown
Masters of American Piano Music (Hinson ed.)	Alfred
Masters of Impressionism (Hinson ed.)	Alfred
Masters of the Early Contemporary Period (Hinson ed.)	Alfred

§ Mosaics (Miller ed.)   Sonos
   (98 pages) Intermediate and early advanced compositions which demonstrate 20th-century compositional techniques. Thirty-one compositions representing seven composers.

Music of Our Time   Kjos; Waterloo Music Co.
   Early and Intermediate compositions by Jean Coulthard, David Duke, and Joan Hansen which demonstrate 20th century compositional techniques. E i ght graded volumes.

New Music for the Piano (Prostakoff ed.)	Alfred
The Pianist's Book of Early Contemporary Treasures	Kjos
Ragtime Gems (Jasen ed.)	Dover
Ragtime Rarities (Tichenor ed.)	Dover

§ Ragtime Rediscoveries (Tichenor ed.)   Dover
   (296 pages) As title suggests, 64 original works from an unique assortment of lesser known ragtime composers. Extensive introduction provides excellent background information on the ragtime tradition.

Seven Americans—Seven Compositions for the Piano   Kjos
   by Contemporary American Composers (Banowetz ed.)

Spanish Music from the Old and New Worlds   Associated

§ Supplementary Solos, Vols. I-IV (F. Clark ed.)   Summy-Birchard
   A graded collection of contemporary jazz sounding solos by composers as David Kraehenbuehl, Lynn Freeman Olson, and Jon George. Includes well-known titles such as "Broken Record Boogie" and "Chattanooga Cha-Cha." Excellent material for students in the latter portion of or exiting a piano method.

The Twentieth Century, Vol. IV (Agay ed.)   Yorktown

§ 12 x 11 Piano Music in 20th Century America (Hinson ed.)   Alfred
   12 original compositions written by 11 contemporary composers.

20th Century Americans	Associated
20th Century Composers	Peters
Twenty Ragtime Jazz Classics for Piano	Hal Leonard
Women Composers of Ragtime (Lindeman ed.)	Presser
World's Greatest Ragtime Solos for Piano (Hinson ed.)	Alfred

Young Pianist's Repertoire Series   Frederick Harris
   A new and expanding series of original compositions by contemporary American and Canadian composers. Each volume is devoted to the works of one composer.

Multi-Period Collections and Anthologies

§ Applause!, Vols. I, II (Olson ed.)   Alfred
*(63 and 79 pages) A collection of frequently taught and performed piano solos
representing all style periods. Volume II composers include Musorgsky, Moszkowski,
Pieczonka, Paradisi, and Villa-Lobos.*

§ At the Piano With Women Composers (Hinson ed.)   Alfred
*(65 pages) Fifteen pieces by women composers from thirteen countries. Includes works
by 18th- to 20th-century composers such as Clara Schumann, Amy Beach, Fanny
Mendelssohn Henselt, and Wanda Landowska. Extensive background information is
provided on each composer.*

Baroque to Modern (Hinson ed.)   Alfred

Beethoven to Shostakovich (Anthony ed.)   Presser

§ Beginning Piano Solos (Sheftel ed.)   Fischer
*(160 pages) A comprehensive anthology of 132 entry-level compositions representing 30
different composers.*

The Best of "My Favorite Classics" (Coates ed.)   Warner

Byrd to Beethoven (Anthony ed.)   Presser

§ Celebration Series, 2nd ed.   Frederick Harris
 Introductory Album; Piano Repertoire Albums 1-10
 A Guide for Students (8 vols.)
 *(Volumes range from 32 to 144 pages.) A carefully graded collection of solo literature
ranging from late elementary to early advanced compositions. Each repertoire album
represents contrasting style periods and incorporates careful editing. The easy to use
guides for students provide learning resource materials for repertoire in the Piano
Repertoire Albums 1-8. Each guide offers information about the pedagogical and
analytical aspects of the piano repertoire and includes composers' biographies and specific
practice suggestions for each piece. Cassette tapes are available.*

Classics Romantics Moderns (Sheftel ed.)   Fischer

More Classics Romantics Moderns (Sheftel ed.)   Fischer

Classics to Moderns Series (Agay ed.)   Consolidated
 Easy Classics to Moderns
 More Easy Classics to Moderns
 Classics to Moderns in the Intermediate Grades
 Early Advanced Classics to Moderns

The Complete Piano Player Collection, II, III (Zeitlin ed.)   Wise

§ Creme de la Creme (Sheftel ed.)   Alfred
*(32 pages) Thirty frequently performed early intermediate piano pieces representing 16
composers from Bach to Bartók. These pieces provide an inviting introduction to the
classical repertoire. A cassette tape or MT100 disc is available.*

§ The Easiest Sonatina Album (Aubry ed.)   Frederick Harris
*(40 pages) A collection of 11 early intermediate sonatinas compiled and graded by Leon
Aubry. Composers include Beethoven, Biehl, Gurlitt, Lichner, Spindler, and Wagner.*

Easy Keyboard Music Ancient to Modern (Palmer ed.)   Alfred

§ Encore!, Vols. I-III (Magrath ed.)   Alfred
(64, 63, and 87 pages) Each volume contains approximately 20 piano compositions organized chronologically by style period. A suggested order of progressive difficulty is included. Cassette tapes are available.

§ Essential Keyboard Repertoire (Olson ed.)   Alfred
(143 pages) Includes 100 early level piano selections (baroque to modern) in chronological order. Twelve selections are identified as easier to assign first.

§ More Essential Keyboard Repertoire (Olson ed.)   Alfred
(142 pages) A sequel to Essential Keyboard Repertoire, this volume includes 75 slightly more difficult compositions.

Essential Keyboard Repertoire Requiring a Hand Span of an Octave or Less (Hinson ed.)   Alfred
(161 pages) Eighty-three intermediate selections in their original form. Pieces are arranged in three levels: Early Intermediate, Intermediate, and Late Intermediate. This volume is designed for students with a small hand.

§ Essential Keyboard Sonatinas, Vols. I-III (Olson/Hilley eds.)   Alfred
(152 pages) Sixteen popular sonatinas from contrasting style periods in their original form. Includes sonatinas of Haydn, Clementi, Diabelli, Kuhlau, Gurlitt, Bartók, and Kabalevsky.

§ Intermediate Essential Keyboard Repertoire (Hinson ed.)   Alfred
(128 pages) An anthology designed specifically for the intermediate piano student. Selection of repertoire was based on interesting melodies and rhythmic patterns, technical accessibility, formal structure, and exceptional aesthetic value. The 85 pieces are arranged in three categories: Early Intermediate, Intermediate, and Late Intermediate. Includes lesser known composers such as Niels Gade, Valentin Rathgeber, and Domenico Zipoli.

Everybody's Perfect Masterpieces, Vols. I-IV (Bigler/Lloyd-Watts eds.)   Alfred

§ Exploring Piano Literature (Olson ed.)   Fischer
§ Exploring More Piano Literature (Olson ed.)   Fischer
(48 pages each) These two volumes contain late elementary entry level solos appropriate for students just completing a piano method. Detailed practice suggestions accompany each composition.

Favorite Classics (Lancaster/Renfrow eds.)   Alfred

First Piano Repertoire Album (Bastien ed.)   Kjos

First Steps in Keyboard Literature (Olson ed.)   Alfred

Four Centuries of Keyboard Music, Vols. II, III   Boston

French Piano Music: An Anthology (Philipp ed.)   Dover

From Bach to Bartók, Vols. 1A, 1B, 1C (Agay ed.)   Warner

Great English Piano Works (Tucker ed.)   Belwin

Great French Piano Works (Tucker ed.)   Belwin

Great German Piano Works (Tucker ed.)   Belwin

Great Russian Piano Works (Tucker ed.)   Belwin

Great Spanish Piano Works (Tucker ed.)   Belwin

Guild Repertoire (Allison/Davidson/Podolsky/Schaub eds.)   Summy-Birchard
    Elementary A, B, C, D
    Intermediate A, B, C, Preparatory A

Harris Festival Series, Levels 1-8   Frederick Harris

Introduction to the Masterworks (Palmer/Lethco eds.)   Alfred

Introduction to Theme & Variations (Halford ed.)   Alfred

The Joy of Classics (Agay ed.)   Yorktown

The Joy of First Classics (Agay ed.)   Yorktown

The Joy of French Piano Music (Agay ed.)   Yorktown

The Joy of Recital Time (Agay ed.)   Yorktown

The Joy of Russian Piano Music (Agay ed.)   Yorktown

Leichte Klavierstücke, Vols. I, II   Henle

Leichte Klaviervariationen   Henle

§   Mainstreams in Literature: Classical Pianist, Performer, Patterns A, B, C   Heritage
    (Noona, Walter and Carol eds.)
    This intermediate level series includes three books at each level. The PIANIST books
    include repertoire and discovery sheets; the PERFORMER books contain additional
    repertoire at corresponding levels; the PATTERNS books are workbooks in style, history,
    form, analysis, composition, and general musicianship.

§   Masterwork Classics, Vols. I-VI (Magrath ed.)   Alfred

§   Practice and Performance, Vols. I-VI (Magrath ed.)   Alfred
    (Volumes range from 32 to 88 pages in length.) Compositions in the Masterwork series
    are selected from Alfred piano editions. Each volume contains 30-40 pieces divided
    among the four style periods. The Practice and Performance volumes contain practice
    suggestions for repertoire in the Masterwork Classics series. Practice suggestions center
    on three stages: preparation, playing, and evaluating. Cassette tapes are available.

Music by the Masters (Lanning ed.)   Musicord

§   Music Pathways Repertoire Series: Books 3A, 3B, 4A, 4B, 5A, 5B   Fischer
    (Volumes range from 32 to 48 pages in length.) This intermediate level series includes
    three books at each level: REPERTOIRE, MUSICIANSHIP and TECHNIQUE. The
    series includes music from the early intermediate through late intermediate levels.
    Concepts in the TECHNIQUE and MUSICIANSHIP volumes reinforce the
    REPERTOIRE books. Levels 5A-B represent upper intermediate compositions.

§   Piano Literature of the 17th, 18th, & 19th Centuries,
    Vols. I-VIB (F. Clark ed.)   Summy-Birchard
    (Volumes range from 24 to 64 pages.) One of the first published collections of carefully
    graded teaching pieces focusing on intermediate level solo piano literature. These
    repertoire books are companion volumes to the Contemporary Piano Literature series.

Piano Literature, Vols. I-IV (Bastien ed.)   Kjos

Piano Literature, Vols. I-IV (Glover/Hinson eds.)   Belwin

Piano Repertoire Series, Vols. I-VI (Kraehenbuehl ed.)   Keyboard Arts

Premier Recital, Vols. I-III   Salabert

Rainbow Collections of Piano Favorites (Wills ed.)	Schirmer
The Blue Book (early intermediate)	
The Yellow Book (late intermediate)	
The Orange Book (sonatinas)	
The Purple Book (late intermediate)	
Schubert to Shostakovich (Anthony ed.)	Presser
7 Centuries of Keyboard Music (Palmer ed.)	Alfred
Sonatinas (varied styles and levels), Vols. I, II (M. Clark ed.)	Myklas
Standard Piano Classics (Small ed.)	Alfred
Themes from Masterworks	Summy-Birchard
World Famous Piano Pieces	Frederick Harris

Holiday Literature

Elementary and Early Intermediate Levels

A Christmas Gathering (Olson) (Includes parts for other instruments.)	Fischer
A Creative Christmas (Rocherolle)	Kjos
A Festival of Folk Carols (Poe)	Kjos
A Musical Christmas for Easy Piano (L. Evans)	Marks
A Razzle Dazzle Christmas (L. Evans)	Hal Leonard
§ A Very Merry Christmas (Younger)	Frederick Harris
§ A Young Pianist's First Christmas (Gillock)	Willis
Carols by Candlelight (Yeager)	Kjos
Celebrations, Book I (C. Shaak)	Moonstone Press
Children's Favourite Christmas Carols (Willan)	Frederick Harris
Christmas Carols for Beginners (Blake/Capp)	Boosey & Hawkes
Christmas Favorites, II (Bastien)	Kjos
Christmas Festival, Vols. I-III (Kowalchyk/Lancaster)	Alfred
Christmas Music, II (Glover/Garrow)	Belwin Mills
Christmas Together (Grill)	Kjos
Easy Christmas Carols (Kern)	Hal Leonard
Easy Christmas Favorites (Kern)	Hal Leonard
Easy Solos for Christmas (Younger)	Frederick Harris
First Favorite Christmas Carols (Olson)	Alfred
§ Happy Holidays! (Olson)	Fischer
Merry Christmas!, Levels 1A-5 (Palmer, Manus, Lethco)	Alfred
My Favourite Christmas Carols	Frederick Harris
My First Christmas Carols (Kowalchyk/Lancaster)	Alfred
§ Songs for Christmas and Hanukah, Books 1, 2 (Kraehenbuehl)	Keyboard Arts
Together at Christmas (Konowitz)	Alfred
World Famous Christmas Carols (Berlin)	Frederick Harris

Intermediate Level

§ A Charlie Brown Christmas (Guaraldi) [out of print]	Felfar
A Christmas Collection, Books 1, 2 (Renfrow)	Alfred
§ A Christmas Pageant (Waxman)	Galaxy
Amahl and the Night Visitors for Easy Piano (Menotti)	Schirmer
Christmas Anew (Rocherolle)	Kjos

§	Christmas Around the World (Rocherolle)	Kjos
	Christmas Carols, Book 3 (Noona)	Heritage
	Christmas Holiday (Palmer)	Alfred
	Christmas Impressions (Rollin)	Alfred
	Christmas Improvisations (Vandall)	Myklas
§	Christmas Miniatures (Vandall)	Bradley
	Christmas Seasonings (O'Hearn)	Kjos
	Christmas Silhouettes (Alexander)	Alfred
	Christmas Songs and Solos (Goldston)	Alfred
	Christmas with Style (Ray)	Alfred
	The Pianist Performs at Christmas-Intermediate (Beard)	Willis
	Simply Christmas (Ray)	Alfred
	Something Special for Christmas (Hartsell)	Alfred
	Sounds Christmas (Olson)	Alfred
	Yuletide Cheer (Rocherolle)	Kjos

Advanced Level

	Appalachian Christmas Carols (Persichetti)	Elkan-Vogel
§	Christmas Around the Piano (Rocherolle)	Kjos
§	Christmas Music (Dello Joio)	Marks
	Christmas Stylings-Modern & Bright, Vols. I, II (Aaronson)	Alfred
	Christmas Tree, Vols. I, II (Liszt)	Hinrichsen-Peters
	Improvisations on 5 Christmas Carols (Norton)	Universal
§	Jazz Up Your Christmas (L. Evans)	Marks
	Jesu, Joy of Man's Desiring (Bach arr. Hess)	Oxford
§	Sleigh Ride (Anderson)	Belwin

ENSEMBLE LITERATURE

Music for One Piano-Four Hands

	Composer Title	Publisher

Agay, Denes (born 1911) U.S.A. (born Hungary)

I	Boogie Variations on Shortnin' Bread	Music Sales
I	Dance Toccata	Sam Fox
I	Ragtime Duets	Hal Leonard

Aitken, Hugh (born 1924) U.S.A.

I	Four Pieces	Elkan-Vogel

Akimenko, Fyodor Stepanovich (1876-1945) Ukraine

I-A	Six Pieces Ukrainiennes Op. 71	Salabert

Albéniz, Isaac (Manuel-Francisco) (1860-1909) Spain

A	Sevilla	Hal Leonard

Alexander, Dennis (U.S.A.)

I	Festival in Cordoba	Alfred
I	Festival Overture	Alfred
I	Valse Caprice	Alfred

André, Johann Anton (1775-1842) Germany

I	Divertimento in A Minor	Peters
I	Six Sonatinas Op. 45 (Hinson ed.)	Alfred

Arensky, Anton Stepanovich (1861-1906) Russia

I	Six Children's Pieces Op. 34 (Philipp ed.)	International
I	Six Pièces Enfantines Op. 34	Leeds
I-A	Twelve Pieces Op. 66 (in 4 volumes)	Jürgenson

Arnell, Richard (Anthony Sayer) (born 1917) England

A	Sonatina Op. 61	Schott

Atkinson, Condit

I	Duet of the Month Club	Galaxy
I	It Still Takes Two (Stecher/Horowitz/Gordon eds.)	Schirmer

Auric, Georges (1899-1983) France

I	Five Bagatelles	Heugel

Averre, Dick

E	Rag-Weed Rag	Belwin

Bach, Johann Christian (1735-1782) Germany
(Johann Sebastian Bach's youngest son)

I	Rondo in F Major	Schott
I	Sonata in C Op. 18 No. 5; Sonata in A	Peters
I	Three Sonatas (Op. 15 No. 6; Op. 18 No. 5; Op. 18 No. 6)	Peters

Bach, Johann Sebastian (1685-1750) Germany

I		A Mighty Fortress	Myklas
I		Bist Du Bei Mir (M. Clark)	Myklas
I		Bourrée (Brady)	Myklas
I		Five Two Part Inventions (Riegger arr.)	Harold Flammer
I		Gavotte Rondo (M. Clark)	Myklas
I		In Sweet Jubilation	Myklas
I		J.S. Bach Chorales for Piano Duet (Bovet arr.)	Galaxy
I	§	Jesu, Joy of Man's Desiring (Gillock)	Willis
I		Sheep May Safely Graze (Howe arr.)	Oxford
I-A		Suites	Kalmus
A	§	Jesu, Joy of Man's Desiring (Hess arr.)	Oxford

Bach, Wilhelm Friedrich (1759-1827) Germany
(The last male descendant in the Bach line)

I	Andante in A Minor	Associated; Schott

Bacon, Ernst (1898-1990) U.S.A.

I	Sassafras	Lawson-Gould

Badings, Henk (born 1907) Netherlands (born Java)

A	Arcadia Books	Schott

Barber, Samuel (1910-1981) U.S.A.

A	§	Souvenirs Ballet Suite Op. 28	Schirmer

Baumer, Cecil

E	Five Duets for Young Fingers	Schirmer

Bavicchi, John (born 1922) U.S.A.

I	A Duet Dozen	Oxford

Beard, Katherine (U.S.A.)

I	Carillon, Great Pealing of Bells	Willis
I	Carnival	Boston
I	Fiddle Fancy	Willis

Beeson, Jack (born 1921) U.S.A.

I		Round & Round	Oxford

Beethoven, Ludwig van (1770-1827) Germany

I	§	Contredanse	Presser
I		March and Gavotte Op. 45	Schott
I		Six Country Dances	Myklas
I		Sonata in D Major Op. 6	Schott
I		Three Marches Op. 45	International
I-A		All Original Compositions (Complete)	International
I-A		Dances (Kirchner)	Peters
I-A		German Dances	Peters; Schott
I-A		Original Compositions (2 volumes)	Peters
I-A		Works for Piano 4 Hands	Henle
A		Grand Fugue Op. 134	Henle
A		String Quartets (Complete)	Dover
A		Variations in C Major	International
A		Variations in D Major	International

Behr, Franz (1837-1898) Germany

I	Snow Drops	Schirmer

Bennett, Richard Rodney (born 1936) England

I	Capriccio	Universal

Berens, J. Hermann (1826-1880) Germany

I	Melodious Exercises Op. 62	Kalmus

Berkeley, Lennox (1903-1989) Great Britain

A	Palm Court Waltz	Chester; Marks
A	Sonatina	Chester; Marks

Berners, Lord (Sir Gerald Tyrwhitt Wilson Bart) (1883-1950) England

I	Three Pieces	Masters
A	Valses Bourgeoises	Chester

Bhatia, Vanraj

I	Indian Nursery	Novello

Binet, Frederic

I-A	Pour déchiffrer	Durand

Bizet, Georges (Alexander César Léopold) (1838-1875) France

I-A		Bizet (Frickert)	Peters
I-A	§	Jeux d'Enfants Op. 22 (Children's Games)	International
A		L'Arlésienne Suites Nos. 1, 2	Kalmus

Böhm, Karl (1894-1981) Austria

I	Attaque des Uhlans, Galop	Schirmer

Borodin, Alexander Porfir'yevich (1833-1887) Russia

I	Polka in D Major	Leeds
A	Tarantelle in D Major (1862)	Leeds

Bortz, Alfred

I-A	Sonata Op. 22	Simrock

Brahms, Johannes (1833-1897) Germany

I	§	Liebeslieder Waltzes Opp. 52, 65 (Mandyczewski ed.)	Henle; Schirmer
I-A		Complete Piano Works for Four Hands	Dover
I-A		Hungarian Dances, Vols. I, II	Henle; Peters; Schirmer
I-A	§	Waltzes Op. 39	Henle; Schirmer; Weiner Urtext
A		Souvenir de la Russie	Karl Dieter Wagner
A		Ten Variations on a Theme by Robert Schumann Op. 23	Peters

Braithwaite, Henry (1896-1971) New Zealand

I	Pastorale	Augener

Brandse, William

I	Double Dutch (Stecher/Horowitz/Gordon eds.)	Schirmer

Brown, Rayner (born 1912) U.S.A.

I	Variations for Four Hands	Western International

Bruch, Max (Christian Friedrich) (1838-1920) Germany

I-A	Swedish Dances Op. 63 (in 2 books)	Simrock

Bruckner, (Joseph) Anton (1829-1896) Austria

E	Three Little Pieces	Oxford; Schott
I	Quadrille (1854)	Heinrichschofen

Burney, Charles (1726-1814) England

I-A	Sonata	Schott

Busoni, Ferruccio (Dante Michelangelo Benvenuto) (1866-1924) German-Italian

I		Finnish Folk Tunes Op. 27	Peters
I		Two Finnish Dances	Peters

Caramia, Tony (born 1950) U.S.A.

I	§	Four By Four (Jazzy Piano Duets)	Belwin
I		Rag Times Four	Kjos

Carleton, Nicholas (circa 1570-1630) England

I	A Verse for Two to Play	Schott

Casella, Alfredo (1883-1947) Italy

I-A	§	Pupazzetti (1916)	Chester
A		Fox-Trot (1920)	Universal
A		Pagine di Guerra (1915)	Ricordi

Chabrier, (Alexis-) Emmanuel (1841-1894) France

I-A	Cortège Burlesque	M. Baron
I-A	Souvenir de Munich	Associated; Presser

Cheadle, William

E-I	Souvenir of Scotland & Somewhere In France	Myklas
I	Camel Train	Myklas
I	Old Fiddler	Myklas
I	Picture Postcards 1, 2	Myklas
I	Russian Santa	Myklas

Chopin, Frédéric François (1810-1849) Poland
(Fryderyk Franciszek)

A	Variations in D – on a Theme by Thomas Moore	Chopin Institute

Clark, Mary E. (U.S.A.)

E-I	Dry Bones	Myklas
I	Rondena Malagueña	Myklas
I	Three Spanish Dances	Myklas
I	Viennese March (Theodor Schrammel)	Myklas

Clarke, Lucia (U.S.A.)

I	Jazz Duet 2	Myklas
I	Rendezvous	Myklas
I	Seldom Blue	Myklas
I	Three Jazz Duets	Myklas

Clementi, Muzio (1752-1832) England (born Italy)
(Keyboard player, publisher, and piano manufacturer)

I	Sonatinas Op. 14 No. 1-2	Ricordi
I	Two Duettino	Schirmer
I-A	Clementi (Ruthardt)	Peters
A	Sonatas	Peters
A	Three Rondos	Schirmer

Cohan, George Michael (1878-1942) U.S.A.

I	Give My Regards to Broadway (Lyke arr.)	Belwin
I	Yankee Doodle Boy (M. Clark arr.)	Myklas
I	You're A Grand Old Flag (M. Clark arr.)	Myklas

Corelli, Arcangelo (1653-1713) Italy

I	Gigue (Gunther)	Belwin

Corigliano, John Paul (born 1938) U.S.A.

A	Gazebo Dances	Schirmer

Crawley, Clifford (born 1930) Canada

I-A	Four Uneasy Pieces	Frederick Harris

Cui, César (1835-1918) Russia

E-I	Ten Pieces for Five Keys Op. 74 (2 books)	Leeds

Curwin, Clifford

I	Six French Nursery Songs	Chester; Marks

Czerny, Carl (1791-1857) Austria

I	Sonatina Op. 156 No. 2 (Weekley / A rganbright eds.)	Kjos
A	Sonatina Brillante Op. 50 No. 1	Presser

Danzi, Franz Ignaz (1763-1826) Germany

A	Sonata	Amadeus

Davie, Roberta (U.S.A.)

I	May Day Carol	Myklas

Debussy, (Achille-) Claude (1862-1918) France

E-I	Golliwogg's Cake Walk (Charlot)	Durand
E-I	Le petite nègre (Delvincourt)	Leduc
I	Le Triomphe de Bacchus	Choudens
I-A	Arabesque No. 1 (arr.)	Durand

I-A		Clair de Lune (arr.)	Boston; Elkan-Vogel
I-A		March Écossaise (sur un thème populaire) (1891)	Jobert
I-A	§	Petite Suite (1889) (Hinson ed.)	Alfred
I-A	§	Petite Suite (1889) (Weekley/Arganbright eds.)	Kjos
A		Six Épigraphes Antiques (1914)	Durand; Marks
A		Works for Piano-Four Hands and Two Pianos, Books 1, 2	Dover

DeCoursey, Ralph

I	The Blue Pagoda	Schirmer

Delibes, (Clement Philibert) Leo (1836-1891) France

I	Mazurka from Coppelia (M. Clark ed.)	Myklas

Delius, Frederick [Fritz] (Theodore Albert) (1862-1934) England

I	A Song before Sunrise (Heseltine ed.)	Augener

Dello Joio, Norman (born 1913) U.S.A.

E	§	Family Album	Marks
I		Five Images	Hal Leonard; Marks
I		Song At Springtime	Schirmer
A		Stage Parodies	Associated; Schirmer

Del Tredici, David (born 1937) U.S.A.

I-A	Scherzo for Piano	Boosey & Hawkes

Demarest, Anne Shannon (U.S.A.)

E	Bouncing Balls	Myklas
E	Caprice	Myklas
I	Simoon	Myklas

Diabelli, Anton (1781-1858) Austria

E		Jugendfreuden (Student/Teacher)	Peters
E	§	Melodious Pieces on Five Notes Op. 149 (Student/Teacher)	Alfred; Belwin; Schirmer
E	§	Pleasures of Youth Op. 163 (Student/Teacher)	Schirmer
I		Five Sonatinas Opp. 24, 54, 58, 60	Peters; Schirmer
I		Rondeau Militaire	Kalmus
I		Sonatas Mignonnes - Rondeau Militaire	Alfred; Kalmus
I		Three Sonatas Opp. 32, 33, 37	Peters; Schirmer
A		Sonatas Opp. 38, 73	Kalmus; Peters

Dichler, Josef

I	3 Kinderszenen	Doblinger

Diercks, John (born 1927) U.S.A.

I-A   Suite No. 1   Music Corp. of America

Dietrich, Karl

A   Prokofiev Variations   Neue Musik

Dohnányi, Ernö [Ernst von] (1877-1960) Hungary

I	Walzer Op. 3	Doblinger
A	Variations on a Nursery Rhyme	Simrock

Donizetti, (Domenico) Gaetano (Maria) (1797-1848) Italy

E-A	Complete Works for Four Hands (22 volumes)	Boccaccini & Spada
I-A	Sonatina in Re Maggiore	Presser
A	Sonatas	E. C. Kerby
A	Three Pieces	Ricordi

Dring, Madeleine (1923-1977) Great Britain

I   Four Duets   Schirmer

Ducelle, Paul

I   Musical Memories Op. 16   Schirmer

Durey, Louis (1888-1979) France

A   Deux Pièces Op. 7 (1916, 1918)   Salabert

Dussek, Jan Ladislav (1760-1812) Bohemia

I-A	Sonata in C Major Op. 43	Mercury
A	Three Sonatas Op. 67	Elkan-Vogel

Dvořák, Antonín (Leopold) (1841-1904) Czechoslovakia

I-A	Legends Op. 59 (2 books)	Mercury
I-A	Selected Pieces	Peters
I-A	Six Ecossaises Op. 41	Schirmer
I-A §	Slavic Dances Opp. 46 and 72, Vols. I, II	Schirmer; Simrock
A	Bagatelles Op. 47	Associated
A	From the Bohemian Forest Op. 68	Simrock
A	Humoreske in G Op. 101 No. 7	Music Sales; Simrock
A	Polonaise in E-flat Major	Peters

Elliott, Robert

I-A   Fantaisie sur un motif de sarabande Op. 3   Novello

Evans, Bill G. (U.S.A.)

E		Mixed Bag	Kjos
I		Jazz Tributes	Kjos

Fauré, Gabriel (Urbain) (1845-1924) France

I-A	§ *	Dolly (Suite) Op. 56 (Berceuse)	Belwin; International; Hamelle

Feldman, Morton (1926-1987) U.S.A.

I-A	Piano Four Hands	Peters

Ferrell, Billie (U.S.A.)

E	Bom Bom Boogie	Myklas
I	Burro	Myklas

Ferroud, Pierre Octave (1900-1936) France

I-A	Serenade (1927)	Durand

Franck, César (-Auguste-Jean-Guillaume-Hubert) (1822-1890) France (born Belgium)

A	Polka	MSM

Frid, Géza (born 1904) Holland (born Hungary)

I-A	Kermesse à Charleroi	Southern

Fuchs, Robert (1847-1927) U.S.A.

I-A	Viennese Waltzes Op. 42, Books 1, 2	Simrock

Gade, Niels (Wilhelm) (1817-1890) Denmark

I-A	Drei Klavierstücke Op. 18	Peters
A	Nordiske Tonebillender Op. 4 (Norwegian Tone Pictures)	Augener

Ganz, Wilhelm (1877-1972) U.S.A. (born Switzerland)

A	Qui vive Grand Galop de Concert Op. 12	Schirmer

George, Jon (U.S.A.)

I	§	Two at One Piano, Book 3	Summy-Birchard
I	§ *	Kaleidoscope Duets (Books 4, 5)	Alfred

Gershwin, George (1898-1937) U.S.A.

I		George Gershwin Piano Duets (Portnoff arr.)	Chappell
A		Cuban Overture	Warner
A		Gershwin Piano Duets	Hal Leonard
A		I Got Rhythm (Stone arr.)	Warner
A	§	Preludes	Warner

Gilbert, Henry Franklin Belknap (1868-1928) U.S.A.

I-A		Three American Dances (Ragtime Dances)	Boston

Gillock, William (born 1917) U.S.A.

I		Boogie Prelude	Willis
I	§	Jazz Prelude	Willis

Glinka, Mikhail Ivanovich (1804-1857) Russia

I-A		Capriccio sur des Thèmes Russes (1834)	Jürgenson

Godowsky, Leopold (1870-1938) Poland

E-I	§	Miniatures (Student/Teacher)	Fischer

Gottschalk, Louis Moreau (1829-1869) U.S.A.

I-A		Music for Piano Four Hands, Books 1, 2	Peer Southern
A		Le Bannanier	Belwin

Graham, Robert

I		Fiddle Tune	Elkan-Vogel
I		Maverick Trail	Elkan-Vogel
I		Shepherd's Suite	Elkan-Vogel

Grainger, (George) Percy (Aldridge) (1882-1961) U.S.A. (born Australia)

I	§	Country Gardens	Boston
I		Let's Dance Gay	Faber
I		Miniatures	Fischer

Gregson, Edward (born 1945) England

E-I		Four Pictures	Oxford

Gretchaninoff, Alexander Tikhonovich (1864-1956) Russia
     (Grechaninov)

E	§	On the Green Meadow Op. 99 (Wolman ed.)	MCA
I-A		Album for 4 Hands Op. 98	Schott

Grieg, Edvard (Hagerup) (1843-1907) Norway

E	§	Norwegian Dances Op. 35 (Nevin arr.)	Peters
I		Elfin Dance Op. 12 (Gunther arr.)	Belwin
I		Peer Gynt Suite Op. 46 No. 1	Peters; Schirmer
I-A		Lyric Pieces Op. 12	MMB
I-A		Norwegian Dances Op. 35 (Original)	Peters
I-A		Wedding-Day At Troldhaugen Op. 65 No. 6	Peters
A		Symphonic Piece Op. 14 No. 2	Schirmer
A		Waltz Caprices Op. 37	Peters

Gurlitt, Cornelius (1820-1901) Germany

I	Beginning Piano Op. 211	Schott

Handel, George Frideric (1685-1759) England (born Germany)

I	Largo	Schott

Hässler, Johann Wilhelm (1747-1822) Germany

A	Sonata VI	Schott

Hauer, Joseph Matthias (1883-1959) Austria

A	Labyrinthischer Tanz	Universal

Haydn, Franz Joseph (1732-1809) Austria

I	Favorite Piano Duets for Beginners	Peters
I	Three German Dances (M. Clark arr.)	Myklas
I-A	Haydn (Ruthardt)	Peters
I-A	Il maestro e lo scolare	Schirmer
A	Partita	Schirmer
A	Twelve Symphonies, Vols. I, II	Peters

Helps, Robert (born 1928) U.S.A.

I	Saccade	Peters

Hindemith, Paul (1895-1963) Germany

A	Sonata (1938)	Schott
A	Ragtime	Schott

Hovhaness, Alan (born 1911) U.S.A. (Armenian heritage)
(Chakmakjian, Alan Hovhaness)

I	A Child in the Garden Op. 16	Peters

Hummel, Johann Nepomuk (1778-1837) Austria

A	Nocturne in F Major Op. 99	Peters
A	Sonata in E-flat Major Op. 51	Peters
A	Variations on a Tyrolean Theme	Schirmer

Husa, Karel (born 1921) U.S.A. (born Czechoslovakia)

I-A	Eight Czech Duets	Schott

Hyson, Winifred Prince (born 1925) U.S.A.

E	Eight Light-Hearted Variations on the Jolly Miller	Kjos
E-I	Our British Cousins	Kjos
E-I	Western Summer	Kjos
I	Fantasy on Three English Folksongs	Kjos

d'Indy, Vincent (Paul Marie Théodore) (1851-1931) France

A	Sept Chants de Terroir	Roicart, Lerolle & Cle.
A	Wallenstein Trilogie	Durand

Ingelbrecht, D. E. (Désiré-Emile) (1880-1965) France

I	§	La Nursery, Books 1-6	Salabert

Jacobson, Maurice (born 1896) Great Britain

I	Mosaic	J. Curwen

Jarnefelt, Armas (1869-1958) Sweden

I	Praeludium	Chester

Jensen, Adolph (1837-1879) Germany

I-A	Drei Klavierstücke	Universal
I-A	Wedding Music	Schirmer
A	Abendmusik Op. 59	Hainauer

Jonbert, John

A	Divertimento Op. 2	Novello

Joplin, Scott (1868-1917) U.S.A.
(Known in the late 19th century as "King of Ragtime")

I		Elite Syncopations (M. Clark)	Myklas
I		The Entertainer	Fentone; Schaum
I	§	Five Joplin Rags (Weekley / Arganbright arr.)	Kjos
I	§	Four Joplin Waltzes (Weekley / Arganbright arr.)	Kjos
I		Ragtime Classics For Piano Duets	Hal Leonard
I	§	Swipesy (M. Clark)	Myklas
I-A		Selected Ragtimes, Vols. I, II	Peters

Juon, Paul (1872-1940) Germany (born Russia)

A	Tanzrytmen (7 books)	Schlesinger

Just, Johann August (1750-1791) Germany

I	Two Little Sonatas	Schott

Kabalevsky, Dmitri Borisovich (1904-1987) Russia

E	Waltz from the Comedians	Willis
E-I	Kabalevsky (Johnson arr.)	Peters
I	Sonatina	Belwin

Kadosa, Pál (1903-1983) Hungary

I-A	Kis Szvit Op. 49	Boosey & Hawkes

Karp, David (U.S.A.)

E	An Ancient Land	Willis
E	The Arkansas Swinger	Willis
I	Dallas Bolero	Willis
I	Dallas Tango	Willis
I	Endless Love	Hal Leonard
I	Two Little Jugs	Belwin
I	Western Bolero	Willis

Kasschau, Howard (born 1913) U.S.A.

I	Famous American Tunes	Schirmer

Khachaturian, Aram Il'yich (1903-1978) Russia

I	Galop from Masquerade Suite	Willis
I	Waltz Masquerade	Schirmer

Koch, Friedrich (1862-1927) Germany

I	Four Dance Episodes	Fischer
I	Golliwog's Dance	Boston

Koechlin, Charles (Louis Eugène) (1867-1950) France

I-A	Quatres Sonatines Françaises	Oxford

Kohn, Karl (born 1926) Austria

I	Castles & Kings (A Suite for Children)	Fischer
I	Recreations for Piano	Fischer

Kolinski, Mieczyslaw (1901-1981) Canada (born Poland)

E-I	First Piano Duets	Schirmer

Krieger, Edino (born 1928) Brazil

A	Sonata	International; Peer Southern

Kuhlau, (Daniel) Friedrich (Rudolph) (1786-1832) Denmark (born Germany)

I		Sonatina in G Major	Schirmer
I	§	Sonatina Op. 17 (Weekley / Arganbright eds.)	Kjos

Kurka, Robert (Frank) (1921-1957) U.S.A.

I	Dance Suite Op. 29	Weintraub

Lambert, (Leonard) Constant (1905-1951) England

I	Trois Pièces Nègres (1949)	Oxford

La Montaine, John (born 1920) U.S.A.

A	Sonata Op. 25	Elkan-Vogel

Lang, Walter (1896-1966) Switzerland

A	Ferientage Op. 64	Amadeus

Lecuona, Ernesto (1896-1963) Cuba

I	The Dolls Have a Party	Hal Leonard
I	Gitanerias	Hal Leonard
I	Merry Go Round Whirl	Hal Leonard
A	Andalucia	Hal Leonard
A	Malagueña	Hal Leonard

Liszt, Franz (1811-1886) Hungary

I-A	Weihnachtsbaum (Christmas Tree)	Breitkopf & Härtel
A	Fest Polonaise	Ricordi
A	Grand Galopp Chromatique (Hofmeister) [out of print]	Breitkopf & Härtel
A	Hungarian Rhapsody No. 2	Ricordi
A	Les Préludes	Schirmer

Low, Joseph (1834-1886) Bohemia

E	Teacher and Pupil, Books 1, 2	Schirmer

Lybbert, Donald (born 1923) U.S.A.

A	Movement	Peters

Lyke, James B. arr. (U.S.A.)

§	"Sing Along" Pop Piano Duets	Belwin
I	Alexander's Ragtime Band (Berlin)	
I	Give My Regards to Broadway (Cohan)	
I	I Love a Piano (Berlin)	
I	It's a Most Unusual Day (McHugh/Adamson)	
I	Play a Simple Melody (Berlin)	
I	Put on a Happy Face (Strouse/Adams)	
I	They Didn't Believe Me (Kern)	

MacDowell, Edward (Alexander) (1860-1908) U.S.A.

I-A	Moon Pictures Op. 21	Alfred
I-A	Three Poems Op. 20	Belwin; Schirmer
I	The Saracens-Aida Op. 30	Breitkopf & Härtel
I	To A Water Lily	Boston

Malipiero, Gian Francesco (1882-1973) Italy

I-A	Armenia	Salabert
I-A	Impressioni Dal Vero	Chester; Salabert

Mana-Zucca [Augusta Zuckermann] (born 1887-1981) U.S.A.

I	Joking	Schirmer
I-A	Four Hand Fancies	Presser

Mason, Daniel Gregory (1873-1953) U.S.A.
(Grandson of Lowell Mason)

I-A	Birthday Waltzes Op. 2	Boston

Masseus, Jan (born 1913) The Netherlands

I-A	Zoological Impressions Op. 24	Peters

Mehegan, John

I	Jazz Caper	Sam Fox

Mendelssohn (-Bartholdy), (Jakob Ludwig) Felix (1809-1847) Germany

I-A	All Original Compositions (Complete)	International
I-A	Favorite Piano Duets for the Beginner	Peters
A	Allegro Brillante Op. 92	Schirmer
A	Andante and Variations Op. 83a	Schirmer

Milhaud, Darius (1892-1974) France

A	Enfantines	Max Eschig
A	La Creation du Monde	Max Eschig
A	Le Boeuf sur le Toit	Max Eschig
A	Suite Francaise	Leeds

Moszkowski, Moritz (1854-1925) Poland

I		Minuet Op. 17 No. 2	Augener
I		From Foreign Lands and Five Waltzes Op. 8	Schirmer
I	§	Spanish Dances Opp. 12, 65	Schirmer

Mozart, (Johann Chrysostom) Wolfgang Amadeus (1756-1791) Austria

I	Andante K. 252 (M. Clark)	Myklas
I	Divertimento K. 213 (M. Clark)	Myklas
I	Leichte Sonatinen	Peters
I	Masterpiece from Symphonic Suite (Perdew arr.)	Myklas
I	Menuetto K. 252	Fischer
I	Polonaise K. 252	Myklas
I	Presto K. 252	Myklas
I	Serenade	Myklas
I	Sonatinas	Peters

I		The Village Musicians	Myklas
I		Viennese Sonatinas	Peters
I-A		Complete Works (Landon/Seidlhofer eds.)	Weiner Urtext
I-A	§	Eine Kleine Nachtmusik	Schirmer
I-A		Fantasy for Mechanical Organ (Badura-Skoda arr.)	Schirmer
I-A		Original Compositions	Peters
I-A		Sonata in C, K. 19d	Oxford
A	§	Six Sonatas; Variations	Henle; International; Schirmer
A		Symphonies & Serenades, Vols. I, II	Peters
A		Twelve Symphonies, Books 1, 2	Schirmer
A		Works for Piano Four Hands and Two Pianos	Dover

Mullen, Frederic

I-A		A Madrid Festival	John Church Co.

Niamath, Linda (born 1939) Canada

E		Outer Limits	Frederick Harris

Niemann, Walter (1876-1953) Germany

I		Koeheler Ländler Op. 135	Peters

Noona, Walter (U.S.A.)

E	§	All American Hometown Band	Heritage
E		Capriccio Chromatico	Heritage
E		El Diablo Cojuelo	Belwin
I		Stamp On It	Belwin

Noona, Walter and Carol (U.S.A.)

E		Spanish Tornado	Heritage

Norton, Christopher (born 1953) U.S.A.

E-I	§	Microjazz Piano Duets I, II	Boosey & Hawkes

Offenbach, Jacques (1819-1880) France (born Germany)

I		Barcarolle (Tales of Hoffman)	Music Sales

O'Hearn, Arletta (U.S.A.)

I	§	Jazz Together	Kjos

Olson, Lynn Freeman (1938-1987) U.S.A.

E		An All-American Gathering (includes parts for other instruments)	Fischer
E	§	Round and Round	Fischer

Onslow, (André) George (Louis) (1784-1853) France

A		Sonata for Piano Four Hands Op. 7	Boonin
A		Sonata for Piano Four Hands Op. 22	Boonin

Ore, Harry

I		3 Latvian Folk Songs Op. 27	J. Curwen

Pachelbel, Johann (1653-1706) Germany
(Bachelbel)

I	§	Canon in D (Weekley/Arganbright arr.)	Kjos

Palmer, Robert (born 1915) U.S.A.

A		Sonata For One Piano Four Hands	Peer Southern

Papineau-Couture, Jean (born 1916) Canada

A		Rondo	Peer Southern

Peaslee, Richard Cutts (born 1930) U.S.A.

E		The Last Bandit	Galaxy
E		The Lopsided Grasshopper	Galaxy

Perdew, Ruth (U.S.A.)

E		Masterpiece Theme	Myklas
I		Gavotte Rondo (Bach)	Myklas
I		Tandem Adventure	Myklas

Persichetti, Vincent (1915-1987) U.S.A.

I	§	Serenade No. 8	Elkan-Vogel
A	§	Appalachian Christmas Carols	Elkan-Vogel

Phillips, Burrill (born 1907) U.S.A.

A		Serenade for Piano	Peer Southern

Pleyel, Ignace Joseph (1757-1831) Austria

A		Sonata in G Minor	Peters

Poulenc, Francis (Jean Marcel) (1899-1963) France

I-A	§	Sonate (1918) [Revised 1938]	Chester

Pozzoli, Ettore (1873-1957) Italy

E	§	Smiles of Childhood (Student/Teacher)	Ricordi
E		Sorrisi Infantili (Student/Teacher)	Ricordi

E	Ten Little Characteristic Pieces (Student/Teacher)	Belwin
I	Piccolo Pezzi Caratt	Ricordi

Prokofiev, Sergey (Sergeyevich) (1891-1953) Russia

E	Gavotte Op. 32, No. 3	Willis
I	Peter and the Wolf (Lauer arr.)	Kjos

Purcell, Henry (1659-1695) England

I	Trumpet Voluntary	Boosey & Hawkes

Quinnell, Ivan

I	Double Delight	Chester

Rachmaninoff, Sergey (1873-1943) Russia
(Rakhmaninov, Sergey, born Semyonov, Russia; died Beverly Hills)

A	§	Italian Polka	Belwin
I-A		Six Pieces Op. 11	Boosey & Hawkes; International
A		Works for One Piano Four Hands	Belwin

Ran, Shulamit (born 1949) Israel

I-A	Children's Scenes for Piano	Fischer

Raphling, Sam (born 1910) U.S.A.

I-A	Four Hand Sonata	General

Ravel, Joseph Maurice (1875-1937) France

I-A		Ma mere l'Oye	Durand
I-A	§	Ma mere l'Oye (Weekley/Arganbright eds.)	Kjos
A		Bolero (arr.)	Durand
A		La Valse (arr.)	Durand
A		Scheherazade	Salabert

Rawsthorne, Alan (1905-1971) England

I-A	The Creel (Suite)	Oxford

Rebikov, Vladimir Ivanovich (1866-1920) Russia

I-A	Petite Suite	Jürgenson

Reger, (Johann Baptist Joseph) Max(imilian) (1873-1916) Germany

A	Cinq Pièces Pittoresques Op. 34	Universal
A	German Dances Op. 10	Schott
A	Introduction & Passacaglia	Breitkopf & Härtel
A	Six Burlesques Op. 58	Schott
A	Six Pieces Op. 94	Schott

A		Variations and Fugue on a Theme of Mozart Op. 132	Peters
A		Waltzes Op. 22	Universal

Reinecke, Carl (Heinrich Carsten) (1824-1910) Germany

A		From the Cradle to the Grave Op. 202	Edward Schuberth
A		Improvisations on a Gavotte from Orpheus Op. 125	Peters
A		Nutcracker and Mouse King Op. 46 (Hinson ed.)	Alfred

Respighi, Ottorino (1879-1936) Italy

A		Six Little Pieces	Associated

Riegger, Wallingford (Constantin) (1885-1961) U.S.A.

I		The Cry	Southern
I		Evocation	Southern
I		New Dance	Southern

Rocherolle, Eugenie R. (U.S.A.)

E		Twice Blessed	Kjos
I	§	Headin' South	Kjos
I		Tierra del Sol	Kjos

Rossini, Gioacchino (Antonio) (1792-1868) Italy

E-I		Petite Fanfare	Curci
I-A		William Tell Overture (Gottschalk/Weekley/Arganbright eds.)	Kjos

Rowley, Alec (1892-1958) England

I		Pastorale	Boosey & Hawkes

Rubinstein, Anton (Grigor'yevich) (1829-1894) Russia

A		Bal Costumé Op. 103	Jürgenson
A		Six Characteristic Pieces Op. 50	Schirmer

Russell, Robert

I		Places	General

Ruthardt, Adolf (1849-1934) Germany

E-I		Teacher and Pupil	Kalmus

Saint-Säens, (Charles) Camille (1835-1921) France

A		Feuillet d'Album	Durand; Elkan-Vogel

Satie, Eric (Alfred Leslie) (1866-1925) France

I		Aperçus Désagréables (1908-1912)	Demets
I-A		Trois Morceaux en Forme de Poire (1903)	Salabert
A		Cinema	Salabert
A		En Habit de Cheval	Salabert
A		La Balle Excentrique	Max Eschig
A		Parade (1916)	Salabert
A		Trois Petites Pièces Montées	Associated

Schickele, Peter (born 1935) U.S.A.

I	§	Little Suite For Summer (Student/Teacher)	Elkan-Vogel
I-A		The Civilian Barber, Overture	Elkan-Vogel

Schoenberg, Arnold (Franz Walter) (1874-1951) Germany

I		Six Pieces	Belmont

Schubert, Franz (Peter) (1797-1828) Austria

I	§	German Dances and Ecossaises Op. 33 (Weekley/Arganbright eds.)	Kjos
I		Serenade	Music Sales
I-A		Easy Original Compositions	Peters
I-A		Marches	Peters
I-A		Marches Originales	MMB
I-A		Original Compositions (4 volumes)	Kalmus; Peters
I-A	§	Original Compositions For Piano, Vols. I, II	Schirmer
I-A		Selected Piano Works for Four Hands	Dover
I-A	§	Works for Piano 4 Hands (Urtext)	Henle
A	§	Fantasia in F Minor Op. 103, D 940 (1924)	Henle; Ricordi

Schumann, Robert (Alexander) (1810-1856) Germany

I	Favorite Piano Duets for Beginners	Peters
I	Kinderball Op. 130	Peters
I-A	Ball-Scenes Op. 109	Peters
I-A	Original Compositions (1 volume)	International; Peters
I-A	Original Compositions, Vols. I, II	Kalmus
I-A	Pictures from the East Op. 66 (Bilder aus Osten)	Peters
I-A	Polonaises	Schott
I-A	Twelve Pieces Op. 85	Peters

Schuster, Giora (born 1915) Israel (born Germany)

I	Mimos I	Israeli Music Institute

Schwalm, Oscar

I	Young Musicians	Kalmus

Scott, Cyril (Meir) (1879-1970) England

I	Three Dances	Presser

Shapero, Harold (Samuel) (born 1920) U.S.A.

A	Sonata for Piano	Mills

Sheftel, Paul (U.S.A.)

I	Duet Yourself	Alfred

Shifrin, Seymour (1926-1979) U.S.A.

I	The Modern Temper	Peters

Shostakovich, Dmitry (1906-1975) Russia
    (Dmitriyevich)

I	Easy Pieces	Schirmer

Shott, Michael (U.S.A.)

I	Duet Preludes	Myklas
I	Nocturne	Myklas
I	Romance	Myklas

Sinding, Christian (August) (1856-1941) Norway

A	Suite Op. 35	Peters

Sousa, John Philip (1859-1932) U.S.A.
    (Known as the "March King")

E-I §	The Marches of John Philip Sousa	Warner
I	Liberty Bell March (M. Clark)	Myklas
I	Stars and Stripes Forever	Warner

Spiegelman, Joel (Warren) (born 1933) U.S.A.

I-A	Morsels	MCA

Starer, Robert (born 1924) U.S.A. (born Austria)

E-I	Five Duets for Young Pianists	MCA
A	Fantasia Concertante (1959)	MCA

Stevens, Halsey (1908-1988) U.S.A.

I	Sonatina for Piano Four-Hands	Helios

Strauss, Johann (1825-1899) Austria
    ("King of the Waltz")

I	Die Fledermaus (M. Clark)	Myklas
I-A	Famous Strauss Waltzes	Schirmer
I-A §	The Waltzes of Johann Strauss	Warner

Stravinsky, Igor (Fyodorovich) (1882-1971)
(Russian composer, later of French (1934) and American (1945) nationality)

E-I	Five Easy Pieces (1917) Easy Primo	Chester; Schirmer
E-I	Three Easy Pieces (1915) Easy Secondo	Chester; Schirmer
A	Petrouchka (revised 1947 version)	Boosey & Hawkes
A	Rite of Spring (Le Sacre du Printemps)	Hansen House

Stravinsky, Soulima (born 1910) U.S.A. (born Switzerland)

E-I	Musical Alphabet, Vols. I, II	Peters

Tansman, Alexandre (1897-1986) France (born Poland)

I	§	Cinq Petites Pièces	Max Eschig
A		Les Jeunes au Piano	Max Eschig

Tchaikovsky, Pyotr Il'yich (1840-1893) Russia

E		Dance of the Sugar Plum Fairy	Willis
E		Polka	Willis
I		Chinese Dance	Boston
I		Sleeping Beauty Waltz (M. Clark)	Myklas
I		Swan Lake (M. Clark)	Myklas
I-A		Fifty Russian Folk Songs	International
I-A		The Nutcracker Suite Op. 71A	Alfred
I-A	§	Russian Folk Songs	Peters
I-A		Tchaikowsky for Two	Willis

Tcherepnin, Alexander (Nikolayevich) (1899-1977) U.S.A. (born Russia)

E	§	Exploring the Piano (Student/Teacher)	Peters
I		Suite Georgienne	Max Eschig

Toch, Ernst (1887-1964) Austria (naturalized American)

A	Sonata Op. 87	Mills

Tomkins, Thomas (1572-1656) Wales

I	A Fancy (16th century)	Schott

Tovey, Sir Donald Francis (1875-1940) England

A	Balliol Dances	Schott

Townsend, Douglas (born 1921) U.S.A.

I-A	Four Fantasies on American Folk Songs	Peters

Turina, Joaquín (1882-1949) Spain

A	La Procession du Rocio Op. 9	Salabert

Türk, Daniel Gottlob (1750-1813) Germany

I-A		Tonstücke für vier Hände, Vols. I, II (Pieces for Four Hands)	Schott

Vandall, Robert D. (U.S.A.)

E		Diamond Sonatina	Myklas
E		Emerald Sonatina	Myklas
E		Seven Canon Duets	Willis
E		Sonatina for Two	Myklas
I	§	Accents for Two	Myklas
I		American Duets	Bradley
I		Black Key Suite	Myklas
I		Brightwood Barn	Myklas
I		Celebration Overture	Myklas
I	§	Festival Suite	Myklas
I		Jubilation	Myklas
I		March Macabre	Myklas
I	§	On the Double!	Bradley
I		Remember When	Myklas
I		Shadow Dance	Myklas
I		Three Waltzes	Myklas
I		Toccata for Two	Myklas
A		Textures	Myklas

Van Gael, Henry

I	Waltz-Lullaby Op. 89	Schirmer

Van Slyck, Nicholas

I	Suite for Four Hands	Willis

Wagner, (Wilhelm) Richard (1813-1883) Germany

A	Polonaise in D Major	Breitkopf & Härtel

Walton, Sir William (Turner) (1902-1983) England

E-I	Duets for Children (2 volumes)	Oxford
I	Two Pieces from "Henry V"	Oxford

Warlock, Peter (1894-1930) England

I	Capriol Suite	J. Curwen

Weber, Carl Maria (Friedrich Ernst) von (1786-1826) Germany

I	Easy Pieces Opp. 3, 10	MMB
I	Invitation to the Dance Op. 65	Fischer; Ricordi
I-A	Pieces for Piano-Four Hands Opp. 3, 10, 60	Peters

Weiner, Leo (1885-1960) Hungary

A	Suite: Hungarian Folk Dances Op. 18	Editio Musica Budapest

Wyk, Arnold van (1916-1983) South Africa

I-A	Three Improvisations on Dutch Folk Songs	Boosey & Hawkes

Wolf, Ernst Wilhelm (1735-1792) Germany

I-A	Sonata in C Major	Schott

Wolf, George Friedrich

I-A	Sonata in F Major	Schott

Woollen, Russell (Charles) (born 1923) U.S.A.

A	Sonata for Piano Duo	Peer Southern

Wourinen, Charles

I	Making Ends Meet	Peters

Yeager, Jeanine (U.S.A.)

I	Have It Your Way	Kjos
I	Times to Remember	Kjos
I	Two Contrasts	Kjos

Zipp, Friedrich (born 1914) Germany

I-A	Canzona e Sonata Op. 22	Schott
I-A	Elmauer Bagatelles	Peters

Collections and Anthologies: One Piano-Four Hands

I-A	Album of Piano Duets (Schmitt ed.), Vols. I, II		Kalmus
I	American Portraits (Penn arr.)		Kjos
I	The Baroque Era		Peters
I-A	Brahms and Dvořák for Two		Summy-Birchard
I-A §	Classical Album (12 pieces)		Schirmer
I-A	Classical Masters		Peters
I	Classics for Two (Weekley/Arganbright arr.)		Kjos
I-A	Duet Classics for Piano		Hal Leonard
I	Duos by the Masters		Schirmer
E-I	Easy 19th-Century Duets		Schirmer
E-I	Easy Original Piano Duets		Consolidated
E-I	Eighteen Original Piano Duets		Schirmer
I-A	Eleven Piano Duets by the Masters (Zeitlin/Goldberger eds.)		Schirmer
E-I	Ensembles for Multiple Keyboards (Carden/Raybuck)		Hal Leonard
I-A	Ensemble Music for Group Piano, Vols. I, II (Lyke ed.)		Stipes
I	Favorite Piano Duets, Levels 3, 4 (Flateau ed.)		Belwin
E	Four American Folksongs (Weekley/Arganbright eds.)		Kjos
I-A	Four Centuries of Piano Duet Music (McGraw ed.)		Boston
I §	Four Hand Music by Nineteenth Century Masters (Ritt ed.) *(267 pages) Includes: Beethoven - Ich denke dein with Six Variations WoO 74; Schubert - Hungarian divertimento Op. 54; Mendelssohn - Andante & Variations Op. 83a; Schumann - Bilder aus Osten Op. 66; Bizet - Jeux d'enfants; Dvořák - 2 pieces; Debussy - Petite Suite; Fauré - Dolly Suite.*		Dover
I-A §	44 Original Piano Duets (from Haydn to Stravinsky) (Eckard ed.) *(159 pages) A collection of easy to intermediate level duets representing 27 composers. Selections include: Arensky - Waltz Op. 34 No. 4; Brahms Op. 39 Nos. 10, 11; Debussy - En Bateau; Fauré - Kitty Waltz; Gretchaninoff - 3 pieces; Moszkowski - Spanish Dance; Weber - Sonatina in C.*		Presser
I	The Great Duets (Bradley arr.)		Bradley
E	Hymns for Two (Weekley/Arganbright arr.)		Kjos
I	Intermediate Piano Duets, Vols. I-V		Peters
E	It Still Takes Two (Stecher/Horowitz/Gordon eds.)		Schirmer
I §	Kaleidoscope Duets, Books 4, 5 (George arr.)		Alfred

E-I	§	Music Pathways, Ensemble-Levels 3, 4, 5 (Bianchi / Blickenstaff / Olson eds.)	Fischer

These three volumes were designed to accompany the Music Pathways Intermediate Repertoire Series - Levels 3A - 5B, but are equally useful with any intermediate level student.

I		Overtures, Vols. I, II	Peters
I	§	Perfect Partners, Vols. I-IV (Johnson arr.)	Fentone

Four volumes of intermediate to upper intermediate duets. Each volume contains four or five duets ranging from Bach to Prokofiev. Selections include: Bach - Jesu, Joy of Man's Desiring; Tchaikovsky - Love Theme; Pachelbel - Canon; Rossini - March from William Tell; Ravel - Bolero.

I		Piano Duets, Books 1-5 (Coates)	Warner
E-I		Piano Duets of the Classical Period	Oliver Ditson
E-I	§	The Pleasure of Your Company, Books 3-5 (Stecher / Horowitz / Gordon)	Schirmer
I		Pops for Pairs (Medley, Bill and Pat arr.)	Hal Leonard
E	§	Primo Light (Weekley / Arganbright eds.)	Kjos
E		Secondo Light (Weekley / Arganbright eds.)	Kjos
E		Primo Profiles (Weekley / Arganbright eds.)	Kjos
I-A		Recital Pieces	Schirmer
I-A		Romantic Masters	Peters
I-A	§	Romantic Piano Duets (Weekley / Arganbright eds.)	Kjos
I-A		Romantic Pieces for Piano Duets	Boosey & Hawkes
I		Sonaten für Liebhaber (Frickert ed.)	Schott
I		Sonatina Album	Peters
I		Style and Interpretation, Volume 5: Keyboard Duets 17th and 18th Centuries (Ferguson ed.)	Oxford
E	§	Three Baroque Pieces (Weekley / Arganbright arr.)	Kjos
I		Three Sonatinas (Weekley / Arganbright arr.)	Kjos
I		Twentieth-Century Composers	Peters
E-I	§	Twice As Nice, Vols. I-III (Weekley / Arganbright eds.)	Kjos
E-I		Two at the Piano (Gruber / Waterman / Harewood eds.)	Schirmer

Holiday Music for One Piano-Four Hands

Early Intermediate

§	Christmas Pageant (Waxman)	Galaxy
	Christmas Together (Grill)	Kjos
	Easy Jazz Christmas (L. Evans)	Marks
	Pat-A-Pan (Vandall)	Myklas

Intermediate

	Christmas Creations (Schaum)	Schaum
§	Christmas Riches (O'Hearn)	Kjos
§	Christmas Side by Side (Rocherolle)	Kjos
§	Duet Fantasy on Jingle Bells (Vandall)	Myklas
	For unto Us a Child Is Born (Handel)	Myklas
	Off We Go to Bethlehem (Davie)	Myklas
	Rise up, Shepherd, and Follow (Vandall)	Myklas
	Russian Santa (Cheadle)	Myklas

Advanced

§	Appalachian Christmas Carols (Persichetti)	Elkan-Vogel
	Christmas Liszt for Two (Weekley / Arganbright arr.)	Kjos
§	Christmas Music (Dello Joio) (Includes arrangements of traditional carols as well as two of the the composer's original carols)	Marks
	Christmas Tree (Liszt) [out of print]	Breitkopf & Härtel
§	Jazz Up Your Christmas (L. Evans)	Hal Leonard

Music for Two Pianos-Four Hands

Composer		Title	Publisher
		Agay, Denes (born 1911) U.S.A. (born Hungary)	
I		The Joy of Two Pianos	Yorktown
		Arensky, Anton Stepanovich (1861-1906) Russia	
A		The Arensky Waltz	Belwin
A	§	Valse Suite Op. 15	Schirmer
		Asch, Anna (U.S.A.)	
I	§	Concertino	Hal Leonard
		Bach, Carl Phillip Emanuel (1714-1788) Germany	
E		Solfeggietto (Van Hulse arr.)	Willis
		Bach, Johann Sebastian (1685-1750) Germany	
E		Ave Maria (Gounod)	Willis
E	§	Bach for Piano Ensemble (Lucktenberg arr.)	Belwin
E		Bach Minuets (Rabinof)	Belwin
E		Sheep May Safely Graze	Boston; Oxford
E	§	Sicilienne (Maier arr.)	Belwin
I		Air on the G String	Willis
I		Badinerie	Boston
I		Concerti in A Major	Peters
I		Fantasia in C Minor	Willis
I		Jesu Der Du Meine Seeles	Galaxy
I-A		Toccata and Fugue in C Minor	Lengnick
		Bach, Wilhelm Friedemann (1710-1784) Germany	
A		Sonata in F Major (Brahms arr.)	Peters
		Bacon, Ernst (1898-1990) U.S.A.	
I		Burr Frolic	Associated
I		Coal Shuttle Blues	Associated
		Bailey, Shad (born 1946) U.S.A.	
I		Joyieux	Myklas
I		Sonata for Two Pianos	Myklas
		Barber, Samuel (1910-1981) U.S.A.	
A		Souvenirs Ballet Suite Op. 28	Schirmer

Beethoven, Ludwig van (1770-1827) Germany

E		Country Dances	Summy-Birchard
E	§	Für Elise (Renfrow/Lancaster arr.)	Alfred
I		Adagio from a Musical Clock	Galaxy
I		Adieu to the Piano	Boston

Benjamin, Arthur (1893-1960) Great Britain (born Australia)

A	§	Jamaican Rhumba	Boosey & Hawkes
A		Two Jamaican Street Songs	Boosey & Hawkes

Bennett, Robert Russell (1894-1981) U.S.A.

I-A	§	Four Piece Suite	Novello
A		Kandinsky Variations	Novello

Berkeley, Lennox (1903-1989) Great Britain

I		Sonatina	MMB
A		Capriccio, Nocturne, Polka	MMB

Berlin, Irving (1888-1991) U.S.A. (born Russia)

I		Alexander's Ragtime Band (Heitler/Lyke arr.)	Belwin
I		Everybody's Doing It Now (Heitler/Lyke arr.)	Belwin
I	§	When The Midnight Choo-Choo Leaves for Alabam' (Heitler/Lyke arr.)	Belwin

Berlioz, Hector (1803-1869) France

A	Romeo and Juliet	Boosey & Hawkes

Bernstein, Leonard (1918-1991) U.S.A.

A	Age of Anxiety	Boosey & Hawkes

Bizet, Georges (Alexander César Léopold) (1838-1875) France

I-A	§	Children's Games	Kalmus

Bloch, Ernest (1880-1959) U.S.A. (born Switzerland)

A	Scherzo Fantastique	Schirmer

Bolcom, William (born 1938) U.S.A.

A	Frescoes	Hal Leonard; Marks

Borodin, Alexander Porfir'yevich (1833-1887) Russia

A	Nocturne (Richter)	Fischer

Boulanger, Nadia (1887-1979) France

A	D'un Matin du Printemps	Schirmer

Brahms, Johannes (1833-1897) Germany

I-A §	Waltzes Op. 39 (Hughes)	Schirmer
A	Variations on a Theme of Haydn Op. 56b	Schirmer

Brandse, William

I	Bagatelle	Schirmer
I	Burlesca	Schirmer
I	Carnival	Schirmer
I	Humoresque	Schirmer
I	Nocturne	Schirmer
I	Overture	Schirmer
I	Rondino	Schirmer

Britten, (Edward) Benjamin (1913-1976) England

A	Introduction and Rondo alla Burlesque	Boosey & Hawkes
A	Mazurka Elegiaca	Boosey & Hawkes
A	Scottish Ballad	Boosey & Hawkes

Casadesus, Robert (1899-1972) France

A	Capriccio	Schirmer

Chopin, Frédéric François (1810-1849) Poland
(Fryderyk Franciszek)

A	Fantasy Impromptu	Fischer
A	Grande Polonaise Brillante	Peters
A	Rondo Op. 73	Peters; Schirmer
A	Variations in D Major	Marks
A	Variations in D Minor	Leonard

Clementi, Muzio (1752-1832) England (born Italy)
(Keyboard player, publisher, and piano manufacturer)

E	Sonatinas Op. 36 Nos. 1-6 (Individual pieces)	Willis
I	Sonatina Op. 37 No. 1	Myklas
I	Sonatina Op. 38 No. 1	Myklas
I	Two Sonatas in B-flat Major Opp. 12, 46	Peters; Schirmer

Cohan, George Michael (1878-1942) U.S.A.

I	Patriotic Cohan, A Medley (Heitler/Lyke arr.)	Belwin

Copland, Aaron (1900-1991) U.S.A.

A	Billy the Kid	Boosey & Hawkes
A	Dance of the Adolescent	Boosey & Hawkes

A	Danza De Jalisco	Boosey & Hawkes
A	Danzon Cubano	Boosey & Hawkes
A	Hoe Down and Saturday Night Waltz	Boosey & Hawkes

Cordero, Roque (born 1917) U.S.A. (born Panama)

A	Duo 1954	Peer Southern

Corigliano, John Paul (born 1938) U.S.A.

A	Kaleidoscope	Schirmer

Debussy, (Achille-) Claude (1862-1918) France

I	Clair de Lune (Gunther arr.)	Belwin
I	Golliwog's Cakewalk	Durand
I Λ	Danses Sacrées et Profanes	Durand
I-A §	Petite Suite (Durand arr.)	Durand
I-A	Prélude à l'après-midi d'un faune	Dover
I-A	Three Nocturnes for Orchestra (Ravel arr.)	Jobert
A	En Blanc et Noir (Swarsenski ed.)	Peters
A	Lindaraja	Jobert

Dello Joio, Norman (born 1913) U.S.A.

A §	Aria and Toccata	Fischer
A	Fantasy and Variations	Fischer

Dohnányi, Erno (Ernst von) (1877-1960) Hungary

A	Valse Boiteuse Op. 39A No. 3	Simrock
A	Valse de Fête Op. 39A No. 4	Simrock
A	Variations On A Nursery Tune Op. 25	Simrock

Durand, Anton

I	Valse in E-flat Major	Willis

Enesco, Georges (1881-1955) Rumania

A	Romanian Rhapsody No. 1 in A Major (Simm arr.)	Belwin

Fauré, Gabriel (Urbain) (1845-1924) France

I	Pavanne	Boston

Feldman, Morton (1926-1987) U.S.A.

A	Intermission 6	Peters
A	Two Pieces (1954)	Peters
A	Projection 3	Peters

Gershwin, George (1898-1937) U.S.A.

A		Cuban Overture	Warner
A		I Got Rhythm Variations	Warner
A	§	Preludes	Warner
A		Rhapsody in Blue	Warner

Gilbert, Henry Franklin Belknap (1868-1928) U.S.A.

I	Three American Dances	Schirmer

Gillock, William (born 1917) U.S.A.

E	§	On a Paris Boulevard	Willis

Glière, Reinhold Moritsevich (1875-1956) Russia
(Reyngol'd)

I	Six Pieces Op. 41	Leeds

Gottschalk, Louis Moreau (1829-1869) U.S.A.

A	Banjo	Schirmer
A	Pasquinade	Belwin
A	Tournament Gallop	Belwin

Grainger, (George) Percy (Aldridge) (1882-1961) U.S.A. (born Australia)

A	Fantasy of George Gershin's Porgy and Bess	Hal Leonard

Gretchaninoff, Alexander Tikhonovich (1864-1956) Russia
(Grechaninov)

I	On the Green Meadow	Hal Leonard

Grieg, Edvard (Hagerup) (1843-1907) Norway

A	Wedding-Day at Troldhaugen	Presser

Handel, George Frideric (1685-1759) England (born Germany)

I	Air From The Faithful Shepherd	Galaxy
I-A	Harmonious Blacksmith	Willis
A	Suite à Deux Clavecins	Oxford
A	Theme and Variations	Belwin
A	Water Music Suite	Oxford

Hanson, Howard (1896-1981) U.S.A.

A	Fantasy Variations on a Theme for Youth	Fischer

Haydn, Franz Joseph (1732-1809) Austria

I	Little Concerto	Boston
A	Toy Symphony	Elkan-Vogel

Hovhaness, Alan (born 1911) U.S.A. (Armenian heritage)
(Chakmakjian, Alan Hovhaness)

I	Ko-ola-u	Peters
I	Mihr	Presser
I	Vijag	Peters

Infante, Manuel (1883-1958) Spain

A	Musiques d'Espagne	Salabert
A	Trois Dances Andalouses	Salabert

Joplin, Scott (1868-1917) U.S.A.
(Known in the late 19th Century as "King of Ragtime")

I	The Entertainer	Willis
I	Maple Leaf Rag	Willis
I	Ragtime for Two Series (Arpin arr.)	Belwin

Kabalevsky, Dmitri Borisovich (1904-1987) Russia

I	Sonatina (Gunther)	Belwin

Kasschau, Howard (born 1913) U.S.A.

I-A	Country Concerto	Schirmer

Kraehenbuehl, David (U.S.A.)

I	Ecossaises	Summy-Birchard
I-A	Marches Concertantes	Fischer
I-A	Rhapsody in Rock	Fischer

Lecuona, Ernesto (1896-1963) Cuba

I	Gitanerias	Hal Leonard
A	Andalucia	Hal Leonard
A	Malagueña	Hal Leonard

Liszt, Franz (1811-1886) Hungary

A	Hungarian Fantasy	Schirmer
A	Hungarian Rhapsody No. 2	Schirmer
A	Rhapsodes Hongroises	Schirmer
A	Spanish Rhapsody	Kalmus

Lutoslawski, Witold (born 1913) Poland

I-A	Variations on a Theme of Paganini	Chester

Milhaud, Darius (1892-1974) France

A	Carnaval à la Nouvelle Orleans	Hal Leonard
A	Kentuckiana	Elkan-Vogel
A	La Bal Martiniquais	Hal Leonard

A	§	Scaramouche Suite	Salabert
A		Suite Française	Hal Leonard

Miller, Dawn Costello (U.S.A.)

E-I		Baroque Mix	Kjos
E-I		Fresh Mix (for electronic keyboards)	Kjos

Moszkowski, Moritz (1854-1925) Poland

I-A		Spanish Dances Op. 12	Schirmer

Mozart, (Johann Chrysostom) Wolfgang Amadeus (1756-1791) Austria

I		Alla Turca	Belwin
I		Sonatina K. 55	Fischer
I		Variations on Ah, vous dirai-je, Maman	Galaxy
A		Adagio and Fugue in C Minor K. 426	Schirmer
A		Don Giovanni Overture	Peters
A		Overture to The Magic Flute (Busoni)	Breitkopft & Härtel
A	§	Sonata in D Major and Fugue in C Minor K. 426	Schirmer

Noona, Walter and Carol (U.S.A.)

I	§	Spanish Tornado	Heritage

O'Hearn, Arletta (U.S.A.)

I	§	Jazz Theme & Variations	Kjos
I		Suite Talk	Kjos

Paderewski, Ignace Jan (1860-1941) Poland

I		Minuet (Palmer ed.)	Willis

Palmer, Robert (born 1915) U.S.A.

I-A		Sonata	Peer Southern

Pancoast, Howard (born 1943) U.S.A.

I		Two Piano Rondos	Myklas
I		Variations for Two Pianos	Myklas

Persichetti, Vincent (1915-1987) U.S.A.

A		Sonata	Elkan-Vogel

Pinto, Octavio (1890-1950) Brazil

I		Scenas Infantis	Schirmer

Poulenc, Francis (Jean Marcel) (1899-1963) France

I		Elegie (1959)	Salabert
A		Aubade	Salabert
A		Capriccio (1952)	Salabert
A		Concert Champêtre	Salabert
A		Sonata (1953)	Chester

Purcell, Henry (1659-1695) England

I		Chaconne on Air "Dido's Lament" (Rabinof)	Belwin

Rachmaninoff, Sergey (1873-1943) Russia
(Rakhmaninov, Sergey, born Semyonov, Russia; died Beverly Hills)

A	§	18th Variation from Rhapsody on a Theme of Paganini Op. 43	Belwin
A		Prelude in C-sharp Minor	Belwin
A		Russian Rhapsody (Hinson ed.)	Belwin
A		Suites Opp. 5, 17	International

Ravel, Joseph Maurice (1875-1937) France

I-A	§	Ma Mere l'Oye	Durand
I-A		Pavanne	Hal Leonard
I-A		Rapsodie Espagnole	Durand

Rebikov, Vladimir Ivanovich (1866-1920) Russia

I		Les Demons s'Amusent	Belwin

Riegger, Wallingford (Constantin) (1885-1961) U.S.A.

I		The Cry	Peer Southern
I		Scherzo	Peer Southern

Rocherolle, Eugenie R. (U.S.A.)

I	§	Waltz for Two Pianos	Kjos

Saint-Säens, (Charles) Camille (1835-1921) France

I		Danse Macabre (Saint-Säens arr.)	Durand
A	§	Le Carnival des Animaux	Durand
A	§	Polonaise Op. 77	Durand
A		Scherzo Op. 87	Durand
A		Variations on a Theme by Beethoven Op. 35	Schirmer

Sanucci, Frank (U.S.A.)

I		Argentinian Rhapsody	Willis
I		Ave Maria	Willis
I		Ballo	Willis
I		Castillian Rhapsody	Willis
I		Danza Español	Willis

I		Danza Mexicana	Willis
I		Rumba	Willis

Schaum, John W. (1905-1988) U.S.A.

I		Birthday Bouquet (Theme and Variations)	Schaum

Schumann, Robert (Alexander) (1810-1856) Germany

I-A		Andante and Variations Op. 46	Peters; Schirmer
A		Six Etudes in Canon Form (Debussy)	Durand

Sinding, Christian (August) (1856-1941) Norway

A		Variations in E-flat Minor Op. 2	Peters

Sousa, John Philip (1859-1932) U.S.A.
(Known as the "March King")

I	§	Marches of John Philip Sousa	Warner

Starer, Robert (born 1924) U.S.A. (born Austria)

A		Sonata for Two Pianos	MMB

Strauss, Johann (1825-1899) Austria
("King of the Waltz")

I	§	The Waltzes of Johann Strauss	Warner

Stravinsky, Igor (Fyodorovich) (1882-1971)
(Russian composer, later of French (1934) and American (1945) nationality)

A		Capriccio	International; Kalmus
A		Madrid	Boosey & Hawkes
A		Movements	Boosey & Hawkes
A		Scherzo à la Russe	Boosey & Hawkes
A		Sonata	Boosey & Hawkes

Tchaikovsky, Pyotr Il'yich (1840-1893) Russia

I		Dance of the Candy Fairy	Schirmer
I-A		Festival Overture	Kalmus
I-A		Four Waltzes (Babin)	International
A		Sonata	Boosey & Hawkes

Vandall, Robert D. (U.S.A.)

I-A	§	Concerto in G Major	Bradley

Walker, George (born 1922) U.S.A.

I-A		Music for Two Piano	MMB
A		Sonata for Two Pianos	MMB

Walton, Sir William (Turner) (1902-1983) England

I   Popular Song   Oxford

Ward, Samuel A. (1848-1903) U.S.A.

I §   America, The Beautiful (Heitler/Lyke arr.)   Belwin

Weber, Carl Maria (Friedrich Ernst) von (1786-1826) Germany

A   Concert Piece in F Minor Op. 79   International
A   Invitation to the Dance Op. 65   Litolf

Weybright, June (U.S.A.)

E   Braziliana   Belwin

Collections for Two Pianos-Four Hands

E-I §   Twice Told Themes   Summy-Birchard

Music for Two Pianos-Eight Hands

Composer	Title	Publisher

Beethoven, Ludwig van (1770-1827) Germany

E	Contra Dance (Seiss/John Thompson)	Willis
I	Adieu to the Piano (Sartorio)	Willis
A	Fidelio Overture Op. 72b	Litolff

Cheadle, William

I	Skip to My Lou and Others Too	Myklas

Dahl, Ingolf (1912-1970) U.S.A. (born Germany)

A	Quodlibet on American Folk Tunes	Peters

Debussy, (Achille-) Claude (1862-1918) France

I-A	Petite Suite	Durand

Dvořák, Antonín (Leopold) (1841-1904) Czechoslovakia

I	Serenade Op. 44 (Morrow)	Fischer

Elgar, Edward (1857-1934) England

I-A	Pomp and Circumstance	Belwin

Gillock, William (born 1917) U.S.A.

I §	Champagne Toccata	Willis

Glover, David Carr (1925-1988) U.S.A.

I	Parade of the Wooden Soldiers	Hal Leonard

Gounod, Charles (1818-1893) France

I §	Waltz from Faust (de Vilback arr.)	Kjos

Grainger, (George) Percy (Aldridge) (1882-1961) U.S.A. (born Australia)

I-A	Country Gardens	Schirmer

Handel, George Frideric (1685-1759) England (born Germany)

E	Three Pieces from Water Music (Carper)	Belwin
I	Allegro Deciso (from the Water Music)	Belwin
I	Two Handel Minuets (from Music for the Royal Fireworks)	Belwin

Moszkowski, Moritz (1854-1925) Poland

I	Spanish Dance, Op. 12	Peters

Mozart, (Johann Chrysostom) Wolfgang Amadeus (1756-1791) Austria

E	German Dance K. 605 (Carper)	Belwin
I	Wind Serenade K. 375 (M. Clark)	Myklas

Purcell, Henry (1659-1695) England

I	Two Trumpet Voluntaries (Carper)	Belwin

Rocherolle, Eugenie R. (U.S.A.)

I	§	Waltz For Two Pianos	Kjos

Schubert, Franz (Peter) (1797-1828) Austria

I	Military March No. 1	Belwin

Smetana, Bedřich [Friedrich] (1824-1884) Bohemia

I-A	Rondo in C Major	Peters

Sousa, John Philip (1859-1932) U.S.A.
(Known as the "March King")

I	§	The Stars and Stripes Forever (Wilberg, arr.)	Kjos

Wilberg, Mack, arr. (U.S.A)

I	§	Sicilienne (Bach)	Kjos
I-A	§	Fantasy on Themes from Bizet's Carmen	Kjos

APPENDIX I

Materials for Adult Instruction

Alexander, Reid and James Lyke. *Exploring Keyboard Fundamentals* (computer tutorial program for adult beginners). Champaign, Illinois: Stipes, 1992.

Allen, Doris R. *Creative Keyboard for Adult Beginners.* Englewood Cliffs, New Jersey: Prentice-Hall, 1983.

Bastien, James W. *The Older Beginner Piano Course* (Volumes I, II). San Diego: Kjos, 1977.

Bastien, James W. and Jane S. *Beginning Piano for Adults.* Park Ridge, Illinois: General Words and Music, 1968.

Chastek, Winifred K. *Keyboard Skills: Sight Reading, Transposition, Harmonization, Improvisation.* Belmont, California: Wadsworth Publishing, 1967.

Chauls, Robert. *Piano for Adults: An Aural Approach.* Los Angeles: Crescendo Publishing, 1984.

Chronister, Richard and David Kraehenbuehl. *Keyboard Arts Adult Music Study.* Princeton, New Jersey: National Keyboard Arts Associates, 1980.

Clark, Frances. *Keyboard Musician - For the Adult Beginner.* Princeton, New Jersey: Summy-Birchard, 1980.

Collins, Ann. *How to Use a Fake Book.* Milwaukee: Hal Leonard, 1985.

Feldstein, Sandy. *Belwin Adult Keyboard Method.* Miami: CPP/Belwin, 1991.

Frackenpohl, Arthur. *Harmonization at the Piano.* Dubuque, Iowa: William C. Brown, 1985.

Giles, Allen *Beginning Piano: An Adult Approach.* Bryn Mawr: Theodore Presser, 1978.

Guhl, Louise. *Keyboard Proficiency.* New York: Harcourt, Brace and Jovanovich, 1979.

Heerema, Elmer. *Progressive Class Piano.* Sherman Oaks, California: Alfred, 1984.

Hilley, Martha and Lynn Freeman Olson. *Piano for Pleasure: A Basic Course for Adults.* Minneapolis: West Publishing, 1986.

Hilley, Martha and Lynn Freeman Olson. *Piano for the Developing Musician* (Volumes I, II). Minneapolis: West Publishing, 1986.

Kern, Alice. *Harmonization-Transposition at the Keyboard.* Evanston, Illinois: Summy-Birchard, 1968.

Lindeman, Carolyn. *Piano Lab: An Introduction to Class Piano.* Belmont, California: Wadsworth Publishing, 1991.

Lyke, James ed. *Ensemble Music for Group Piano* (Volumes I, II). Champaign, Illinois: Stipes, 1976.

Lyke, James; Tony Caramia; Reid Alexander; and Ron Elliston. *Keyboard Musicianship* (Volumes I, II). Champaign, Illinois: Stipes, 1993.

Lyke, James; Denise Edwards; and Don Heitler. *Keyboard Fundamentals* (text for adult beginners). Champaign, Illinois: Stipes, 1991.

Lyke, James and Don Heitler. *First Year Piano Patterns with Rhythm Background* (Cassette Tapes, I, II). Champaign, Illinois: Stipes, 1991.

Mach, Elyse. *Contemporary Class Piano*. New York: Harcourt, Brace, Jovanovich, 1988.

Mainous, Frank D. *Melodies to Harmonize With*. New York: Prentice-Hall, 1978.

Page, Cleveland. *The Laboratory Piano Course* (Volumes I, II). New York: Dodd, Mead, 1974.

Palmer, Willard A.; Morton Manus; Amanda Vick Lethco. *Alfred's Basic Adult Piano Course* (Volumes I-III). Sherman Oaks, California: Alfred, 1987.

Sheftel, Paul. *The Keyboard, Explorations and Discoveries*. New York: Holt, Rinehart and Winston, 1981.

Squire, Russel N. and Timothy P. Shafer. *Class Piano for Adult Beginners*. Englewood Cliffs, New Jersey: Prentice-Hall, 1991.

Starr, Constance and William J. *Practical Piano Skills*. Dubuque, Iowa: William C. Brown, 1992.

Stecher, Melvin; Norman Horowitz; Clair Gordon; R. Fred Kern and E. L. Lancaster. *Keyboard Strategies: A Piano Series for Group or Private Instruction Created For the Older Beginner* (Master Texts I, II). New York: G. Schirmer, 1984.

Swain, Alan. *Four Way Keyboard Systems (Books 1-3)*. Glenview, Illinois: Creative Music, 1977.

APPENDIX II
Listing of Publishers

A. Broude
Alfred Publishing Co.
Alphonse Leduc
Amadeus
American Composers Alliance
    (ACA)
Arcadia Music Publishing Co.
Arrow Press
Artia
Associated Music Publishers
Augener
Bärenreiter
Baron, M. Co.
Boccaccini & Spada
Boosey & Hawkes
Boston Music
Bradley
Breitkopf und Härtel
Broude Brothers, Inc.
Cambria
Carl Fischer
Chappell Music Co.
Chester, J. W.
Chopin Institute Edition
Colombo
Choudens
Colombo, F.
Composers Fasimile Edition
Concordia
Consolidated Music Pub.
CPP/Belwin
Cranz, A.
Crescendo Publishing, Los
    Angeles
Curci
Curwen & Son, J.
Doblinger, Ludwig
Dover
Durand & Co.
E. C. Kerby
Editio Musica Budapest
Editions Aug. Zurfluh
Edward Schuberth
Elkan-Vogel
Max Eschig (ESC)
Faber Music
Felfar Music
Fentone
Ferguson, H.-S & B
Foetisch

Frank Music
Frederick Harris Music Co.,
    Limited
Galaxy Music
General Music Publishing
Hainauer
Hal Leonard
Hamelle & Co.
Hansen House
Hansen, Wilhelm
Harold Flammer
HAS/Henle
Heinrichshofen's Verlag
Helios Music Edition
Henle Verlag, G.
Heritage
Heugel & Cie.
Hinrichsen Edition
Hinshaw
International Music Corp.
Israeli Music Institute
J. Church Co.
Jobert, Jean
Joseph Boonin
Jürgenson, P.
Kalmus, Edwin F.
Karl Dieter Wagner
Kendor
Keyboard Arts
Kjos
Lawson-Gould Music
Lee Roberts
Leeds Music Corp.
Lemoine, Henry
Lengnick & Co., Ltd.
Litolff Collection
M. Baron Co.
MCA Music
Marks Music
Masters
Mercury
MESA Music Press
Mills Music, Inc.
MMB Music
Moonstone
MSM Music
Music Corp. of America
Music Sales
Musicord
Musikwissenschaftlicher
    Verlag Wien

Myklas Music Press
Nagel
Neue Musik
New School for Music Study
New World Music Corp.
Novello and Company, Ltd.
Oliver Ditson
Oxford University Press
Peer International
Peer Southern
Peters, C. F.
Polskie Wydawnictwo Muzyczne
PWM Edition
Prentice-Hall, Inc.
Presser, Theodore
Pro Art
Ricordi & Co.
Ries & Erler
Robbins Music Corp.
Roicart, Lerolle & Cle.
Salabert, Editions
Sam Fox Publishing Co.
Schaum
Schirmer, E. C.
Schirmer, G.
Schlesinger
Schott
Schroder & Gunther
Shawnee Press, Inc.
Simrock, N.
Sonos
Southern Music Co.
Stipes Pub. Co.
Summy-Birchard Co.
Suvini Zerboni
Templeton Publ. Co., Inc
TRO Ludlow
Unión Musical Española
Universal Edition
Warner Brothers Publishing
Waterloo Music Co.
Watson-Guptill Publications
Weiner Urtext
Weintraub Music Co.
Werner-Curwen
Western International
Westwood Press, Inc.
Willis Music Co.
Wise Publications
Yorktown Music Press, Inc.